D1435222

# MINIATURE CARS

Series editor: Frédérique Crestin-Billet
Design: Lélie Carnot
Typesetting by Muriel Lefebvre, Paris
Translated from the French by Anne Rubin, London
Copy-edited by Sandra Raphael
Originally published as La Folie des Autos Miniatures
© 2000 Flammarion, Paris
English-language edition © 2002 Flammarion USA Inc.

ISBN: 2-0801-0718-6
Printed in France

# *Collectible*

# MINIATURE CARS

*Dominique Pascal*

Flammarion

*Close this book immediately or you might well run the risk of falling under the spell of these toys that not so long ago, I am sure, were part and parcel of your daily routine. And rekindling your passion for these green, red, or blue Cadillacs, Ferraris, or Talbots is only a short step away...*

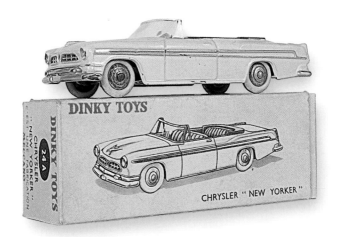

# CONTENTS

# *Introduction*

D o any of us need reminding that
the toy car came into being at the same time
as its life-size model, the real car? And if the
earliest cars were a motorized form of the horse-drawn
carriage, the same was true of their replicas, given that
small boys at play have always wanted to mimic their
fathers down to the very last detail.

Then cars improved in shape. A hood at the front,
a trunk at the back, headlights on both sides, and a
leather steering bar all combined to define the modern
motorcar, finally free of horses. Toys followed these
trends in their appeal and realism. Small boys were
no different.

It should be pointed out that in the early 1900s drivers would first buy a car chassis to which their favorite cartwright or licensed coachbuilder would fit the bodywork, thereby lending the car its intrinsic character and personal touch. In other words, cars were almost all made from the same mold, but with infinite variations. That is why these period generic toys resemble a type of car, without looking specifically like a Delahaye, a Spyker, or a Gaggenau.

*It was the Germans who produced the finest toy cars at the beginning of the century. In fact, they were the first to master the technique of producing flat, lithographed, sheet metal that could then be pressed to form the shape of the toy required.*

*Toys followed the development of cars with a great deal of accuracy, including every detail and every modern improvement, such as acetylene headlamps, wooden wheels, and moleskin seats.*

A nd if I have chosen to mention these particular marques, two of which are completely unknown, it is to emphasize the tremendous variety of automobile firms that existed at the time. They did not see the point of replicating one particular model, since all cars in the street were so different that they all ended up looking alike. On the other hand, children had small-scale models equipped with miniature boilers or tiny batteries that were exact reproductions of their fathers' real-life cars with engines powered by steam, electricity, or petrol.

B efore the First World War, the most beautiful toys came from Germany. In fact it was here that the method for pressing previously lithographed steel was developed. It was by means of this process that brands such as K.B.N., Bing, and Carette manufactured ranges of high-quality toy cars, K.B.N. and Bing both producing their first models in 1904.

Toy cars fell into two categories, the expensive and the cheap. Before the 1914-18 war and for the following twenty years, these cheap nickel and dime toys would be small, simply designed cars made in steel, with sharp edges. Strangely enough, their scale was close to 1:43, which we will discuss later. It was obvious that this format was ideally suited to children who could stuff the cars quickly into their pockets when approached by a rival group in the playground or when about to be reprimanded by a teacher. We cannot leave the subject of cheap toys without mentioning the trade name C.R., standing for Charles Rossignol, who for nearly half a century produced these cheap items in hundreds of thousands, using manufacturing techniques that had become obsolete. It is therefore not surprising that these toys that had outgrown their time did not survive the 1950s.

*Manufactured in lithographed steel between the two world wars, on a scale close to 1:43, these small C.R. cars seem to be the precursors of names such as Dinky, Corgi, and Prämeta.*

The first person to create a car based on its life-sized model was Fernand Migault, in the early 1920s. Indeed, this industrialist was the forerunner of toys that were set to revolutionize the world of the miniature model car and which would become known as Citroën toys. The collector and discerning dealer in this field, Philippe Lepage, summed it up perfectly when he said, "André Citroen was at the forefront of car fetishism." It is clear that by agreeing to give Migault a few moments of his time, he realized what image-boosting benefits he could gain from fashioning his own cars as miniature models. André Citroën, who in France had already invented a famous series and a popular car, also invented car advertising. In the same way as he rented the Eiffel Tower to put his name in lights, thought up slogans, brochures, competitions, and almanacs, or published children's cartoons featuring his cars, so he had Migault draw up exact replicas of the productions that came out of his factory at Javel. The brilliant André wanted the first three words uttered by young children to be "Daddy, Mummy, and Citroën." He certainly knew how to go about it!

The first Citroën toy, replicating a taxi, Type A, was made in wood with metal fenders. Citroën was to produce the B2 some time later, at the end of 1923. This was an all-steel car for towing, which would later be equipped with a motor. Pictured here is a Citroen 5CV, made on a acale of 1:10, also in steel, and fitted with a clockwork motor. It was produced between 1923 and 1926.

Thanks to the relationship between Fernand Migault and André Citroën, miniature cars were to become increasingly detailed and the generic models that were current up to that time were gradually replaced by cars that were faithful replicas of the actual models. Contrary to what is often said on this subject, it is likely that Citroën toys were sold at a loss, for they cost so much to produce. We know that they were manufactured at Briare by the French toy company, Compagnie Industrielle du Jouet, commonly referred to as C.I.J., and not at the Javel factory, as we were led to believe for a long time.

*Reproduction of the record-breaking Rosalie that in 1933 achieved 50,000 miles (80,000 km) at nearly 75 mph (120 km/h). André Citroën could not let this event pass by without taking advantage of the promotional opportunities and he designed this car. On a scale of 1:10, it is 17 inches (43 cm) long and has a clockwork motor.*

They were on sale at Citroën agents and top-of-the-range toy dealers. André Citroën wanted to steer children toward his creations while they were still very young and he certainly managed to do this. In fact, when we see the current television advertising for the Peugeot 806 in Europe—*the car children recommend to their parents*—we cannot help but think of the renowned André who never underestimated just how persuasive little children can be.

In department stores at Christmas time entire windows were devoted to Citroën toys.

*Citroën miniatures were more than just little toys. The Citroennette, in pedal or motorized versions, gave equal delight to children who could glide inside and go off in search of adventure along their garden paths.*

**P**eople could marvel at scenes showing traffic jams, car manufacturing at Citroën factories, and the first trans-African car expedition, known as "the Black Cruise." Children, utterly bemused by all these illuminated displays, could not wait to return home to compose a beautiful letter to Santa written in their best handwriting with their Sergeant Major pens dipped in purple ink. With heads bent and tongues tensed in concentration, they would ask him for this C4 model or that front-wheel drive. The celebrated Citroën Christmas trees also provided magnificent opportunities for offering its brand toys as gifts to the children of employees. It is believed that 800,000 Citroën toys were manufactured and sold between the time Fernand Migault first became involved in 1922 and the eviction of André Citroën from his company. Moreover, it should be explained that when the Michelin family bought Citroën, it put an end to any agreement between the French toy company C.I.J. and the chevron brand, proving that these toys were selling at a loss. This scheme fell neatly into the hands of Louis Renault who took the idea for his own and commissioned C.I.J. to make Renault toys, just as fantastic as the Citroëns!

*Miniature cars had several possible motors, always in line with the technology of their time. The turn of the twentieth century saw motors driven by steam and electricity, but clockwork and rubber-band motors also existed. In these two cases, a key was used to wind the mechanism.*

Jep was a firm that also followed in the footsteps of C.I.J. and Citroën, but it produced cars that were more toys than faithful models, as the Citroëns were. However, their advantage lay in the fact that they resembled other more prestigious marques, such as Delage, Hispano, Rolls-Royce, or Bugatti. The Germans in their turn continued to come up with innovative ideas during the 1930s and flooded Europe with well-made toys. After the Second World War they lost this control to the Japanese who used their infinite powers of creativity to·conquer the market with models replicating American cars, made from lithographed steel. The Italians too produced toy cars in vast numbers. Although their manufacturing process was less spectacular than that of either the French or the Germans, it did involve delicate and skillful work, often reproducing cars such as Fiats and Maseratis that were hailed as Italian champions between the two wars. Cardini and Metalgraf, before the 1940s, then Toschi some time later, produced some remarkable small-scale models of real-life cars. Toschi, in particular, created a large Formula 2 Ferrari, equipped with a motor powered by a rubber band that was activated with a handle located in the radiator grille.

I n Spain the toy capital was Ibi, near Alicante, where two marques of Iberian toys set up their industry and have maintained their fame. Rico, founded in 1916, produced toys including a wonderful Hispano Suiza lorry in lithographed steel, as well as a whole string of motorcycles, using the German method of construction. The other great Spanish brand was Paya, created ten years before Rico. Its Bugatti 35 model, also in lithographed steel, was distributed during the 1930s and relaunched in the mid-1980s.

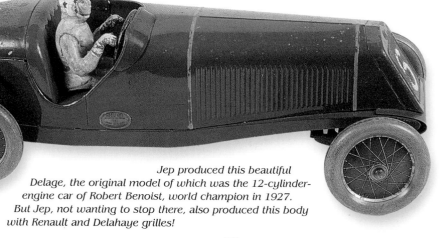

*Jep produced this beautiful Delage, the original model of which was the 12-cylinder-engine car of Robert Benoist, world champion in 1927. But Jep, not wanting to stop there, also produced this body with Renault and Delahaye grilles!*

A s far as American toy cars were concerned, they had the distinctive feature of being very heavy, since American manufacturers used cast steel for mass production. Their weight made the inclusion of any kind of motor impossible. What is more, although these toys were realistic, the way they were made meant that they were not very well finished. However, a few pioneers, like Keystone, produced some extraordinary examples. In fact, these cars were built from sheet metal sufficiently strong to allow children to sit on them if they wanted to. Some manufacturers, such as Louis Marx of Straus Man & Company, New York, copied these toys from Germany by manufacturing lithographed steel cars. As for Tootsietoys, this marque was to make its name as the pioneer in light steel-cast toy cars. In spite of this, young American children long remained fans of first European, then Japanese toys. In 1945, it was Canada and the United States that saw the largest sales of Dinky Toys, and several models were fashioned specifically for these markets.

*This was almost certainly how careers came into being in the mid-1950s.*

# MECCANO

## DINKY TOYS

### 150 Varieties

25F  25B
25D  25C
25E  25A

Meccano Dinky Toys No. 25
**COMMERCIAL MOTOR VEHICLES**
ed with rubber tyres and silver-plated radiators.

| No. 25a | Wagon | ... | ... | each 9d. |
| No. 25b | Covered Van | ... | " 9d. |
| No. 25c | Flat Truck | ... | ... | " 9d. |
| No. 25d | Petrol Tank Wagon | ... | " 9d. |
| No. 25e | Tipping Wagon | ... | " 9d. |
| No. 25f | Market Gardener's Van | " 9d. |

Price of complete set 4/6

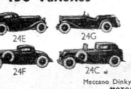

24E  24G  24D  24A
24F  24C  24H  24B

Meccano Dinky Toys No. 24
**MOTOR CARS**
Fitted with rubber tyres and silver-plated radiators.

| No. 24a | Ambulance | ... | ... | each 9d. | No. 24e | Super Streamline Saloon | each 9 |
| No. 24b | Limousine | ... | " 9d. | No. 24f | Sportsman's Coupé | ... | " 9 |
| No. 24c | Town Sedan | ... | " 1/- | No. 24g | Sports Tourer (4 seater) | " 1 |
| No. 24d | Vogue Saloon | ... | " 9d. | No. 24h | Sports Tourer (2 seater) | " 1 |

Price of complete set 6/6

Meccano Dinky Toys No. 60
**AEROPLANES**

| No. 60a | Imperial Airways Liner | each 9d. |
| No. 60b | D.H. "Leopard Moth" | " 6d. |
| No. 60c | Percival "Gull" | ... | " 6d. |
| No. 60d | Low Wing Monoplane | ... | " 6d. |
| No. 60e | General "Monospar" | ... | " 6d. |
| No. 60f | Cierva "Autogiro" | ... | " 6d. |

Price of complete set 3/-

60E  60A  600
60D  60F  60

Meccano Dinky Toys No. 52  **CUNARD WHITE STAR LINER "QUEEN MARY"**
A scale model of the World's largest ocean liner.        Price 1/- each
Meccano Dinky Toys No. 52a.  Exactly as No. 52, but fitted with roller wheels.  Price 1/- each

PRO
MEC
LIVER

50F  50F  50C  50E
50A  50B  50B

S trictly speaking, the toy-car industry, which is the subject of this
book, began its life in England, thanks to a certain Frank Hornby,
who had created the Meccano construction kits in 1899 and had
been manufacturing 0 gauge trains in Liverpool since 1919. Using a scale
close to 1:43, his train engines and cars were charming and well
constructed. In addition to this main activity, he decided to manufacture
accessories to complement his trains. So, to bring his stations to life, he
produced model figures including policemen, porters, young characters
and old, in short, a whole varied population. He also
created animals to watch the trains go by, followed later
by a few cars and lorries. These vehicles were so well
made that he was forced to meet a strong demand
by creating the Dinky Toys trade name in 1934. He
launched a special production line with the result that
his cars sold better than his trains, and that was the
birth of the trend for the "one to forty-three" models.

*Opposite, one of the first catalogues from Dinky Toys,*
*the marketing brand for toys manufactured by*
*Meccano of Liverpool. Eight months after the first cars*
*were unveiled, the Dinky Toys range totaled 150 items*
*and by 1938 that number had doubled.*

## Mazac

As you read through this book you will often come across the word "mazac," referring to the material used in the casting process for miniature cars. Each letter of this amazing word is the label of a different alloy. The M stands for magnesium, A for aluminum, Z for zinc, A for antimony, and lastly C for copper: mazac.

The percentages of each ingredient should be counted as 95. percent zinc and 4.8 percent aluminum, the other components existing only as trace elements, that is, only in tiny quantities. The reason for these homeopathic doses is explained by the properties offered by each of them: copper gives good conductibility to the item, particularly where chromium plating is concerned, and the antimony helps the car to set once it has been removed from its mold and allowed to cool down. These alloys are likely to differ from one marque to another. For example, we know that Dinky Toys used these ingredients in the following proportions: 92 to 96 percent zinc, 3 to 4 percent aluminum, 1 to 2 percent copper, and a trace of magnesium. But caution was needed, for a mere trace of lead in the mazac caused the car to be destroyed beyond repair. This is the fate waiting for some models that will leave no more than a trace of dust in decades to come.

From the mid-1930s, other manufacturers were eager to follow this trend of producing 1:43-scale miniature cars, a phenomenon that developed all the more after the war since raw materials were rare and expensive. Do not imagine for a moment that Meccano was alone in this growing market. There was no shortage of contenders offering children cars made on the same scale, with several of them even choosing a name ending in Toys, to bewilder parents even more. Children, on the other hand, were always smart in this respect. As for the name Dinky, this seems to be of Scottish origin, like Frank Hornby himself, and means "small" or "dainty".

*It is every collector's dream to find a display unit like this one, used by shops to exhibit the latest Dinky Toys in their windows. This hugely dynamic firm also published its own Meccano Magazine, which was around well before Dinky Toys began, since it dates from 1923. The company also created a collectors' club in 1957, the Dinky Toys Club. Each member received a metal badge and a membership certificate signed by Roland G. Hornby.*

**B**etween 1934 and 1979, Dinky Toys, together with several other toy cars on a similar scale, delighted millions of boys—and girls on odd occasions—the world over. Throughout this time, any child receiving a Dinky toy considered it a truly wonderful gift. A good school report, being brave at the dentist's, or facing an injection from the nurse, all these situations could be rewarded with a small yellow box.
Now I would like to take you on a tour of this colorful and familiar universe. I hope that with each page you turn you will feel rewarded, if indeed you failed to be rewarded in your childhood days for all the bravery you showed back then, which had never been properly acknowledged, until now, that is!

# I

## *Miniature*
# SALOONS

**W**hat great family cars they were, these four-door saloons or sedans. We remember them not only as the cars in which our fathers drove us, unwilling as we were, to church on Sunday, but also those that witnessed our first secret attempts at driving. These sedans represented the biggest share of the automobile market, in real life as much as in miniature, and this is still true today. The reason for this is quite simple: when a father bought a real sedan he would often buy a miniature one for his son.

But as children we were oblivious of the history surrounding its various names. Whereas English speakers use the word "sedan", which used to mean a lavish hand-carried chair, or "saloon" derived from the Italian for a large hall, the French use the old English word "berline", which means horse-drawn carriage and comes from "Berlin", the German capital!

*In addition to this sedan, reference number 24 B, the 24 series were the first French Dinky Toys produced over the years between 1934 and 1936. The series included five other models: the town sedan, the super streamlined saloon, the sportsman's coupé, the four-seater sports tourer, and lastly the two-seater roadster.*

*Note the cross-braced chassis on the facing page, typical
of Meccano construction of the time. The wheels are made
of metal and the grille and headlamps are separate castings.*

*There is no chassis for this rare Chrysler Airflow, manufactured by Dinky Toys England. This hollow-cast car, reference number 30 A, was also assembled at Dinky's factory in Bobigny for the French market.*

*The radiator grille and headlamps are separately cast,
then attached to the model after the paintwork is completed. We
should not forget that the Airflow was launched in 1934 and
although it was a wonderful car, almost caused Chrysler's collapse.*

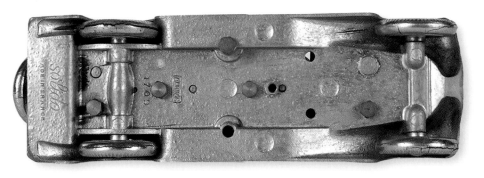

*Created by Solido in 1932, this toy is part of a set
of around 20 cars in kit form. All these toys had parts that
could be exchanged on a common chassis.*

*Just like the other bodies in the range, this is a generic model from the 140 series of 1934, bearing no resemblance to any particular car. On the facing page, notice the mounting bolt under the chassis, holding the bodywork together.*

*The Major or 140 series from Solido appeared in 1932, but this model dates from 1937. The reference number 140 refers to the length of the chassis, which measures 140 millimeters. This car does not represent a specific model, but is in keeping with the style of the period.*

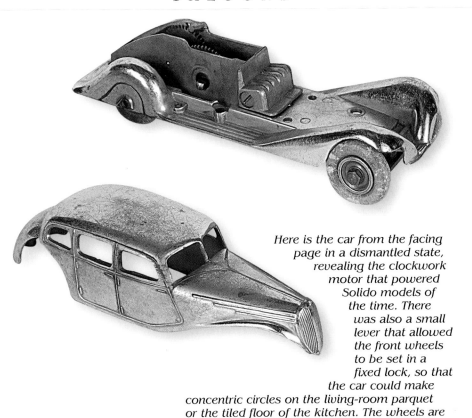

*Here is the car from the facing page in a dismantled state, revealing the clockwork motor that powered Solido models of the time. There was also a small lever that allowed the front wheels to be set in a fixed lock, so that the car could make concentric circles on the living-room parquet or the tiled floor of the kitchen. The wheels are made of rubber.*

*This Dinky 24 P
saloon, issued in France in
1949, was originally a British model.
This time, a sheet-steel base formed the chassis.
This is the Packard Eight Sedan of 1937, not very
common in Europe, but relatively well distributed in
the United States, where in that year alone the Packard marque
sold around 110,000 models at the attractive price of 990 dollars.*

*This Dinky 30 D Vauxhall was introduced without a chassis in 1935, then reappeared after the war in 1948, this time complete with chassis. Notice how the steel axles are nipped at the ends to hold the wheels together.*

*Here is the Dinky Toys 24 K
Peugeot 402 sedan with its metal
wheels, manufactured between 1939 and 1940,
as well as after the war. A taxi version could also be found.
Note that there are separate steel bumpers. To date a car of
this type, it should be noted that prewar models are hollow,
whereas models manufactured after the Second World War
include a sheet-metal chassis.*

*This model,
manufactured in
England just before the war,
is the Dinky Toys 39 E Chrysler Royal
Sedan. Its color schemes were navy blue,
gray, dark green, slate blue, and dark gray, with
wheels always in black. After the war, it was to reappear in
brighter colors, with blue, green, or cream wheels.*

*Released in 1939, like the other American cars in this series, the Dinky Toys Oldsmobile Sedan was allocated reference number 39 B. A much sought-after car, marketed for the first time in 1939, it was reissued in 1946 and then again in 1950. The model pictured here dates from the latter period.*

Manufactured exclusively
in England, the Hudson Commodore
sedan had Dinky Toys reference number
139 B. It was apparently launched in this
two-tone livery of maroon and cream, but
also existed in tan and blue or gray and blue.

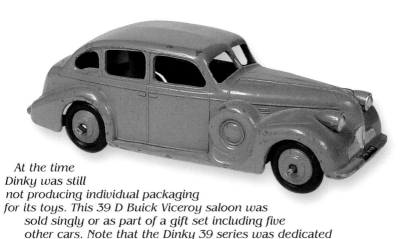

At the time
Dinky was still
not producing individual packaging
for its toys. This 39 D Buick Viceroy saloon was
sold singly or as part of a gift set including five
other cars. Note that the Dinky 39 series was dedicated
to American cars and specifically intended for export to the
United States and Canada.

*This Minialuxe Hotchkiss Grégoire saloon dates from 1954, whereas the full-sized model had been launched three years earlier.*

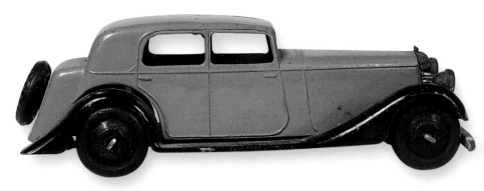

*Do not look for this model in the Dinky Toys list,
because you will not find it. Well, not exactly. This 30 C
Daimler car was adapted by a child, who fitted a spare
wheel to the trunk. It first appeared in 1935, and was
then relaunched in 1948.*

*This Dinky Toys 40 D Austin Devon is a typically British model that started its career in 1949 and was reserved more or less for the British home market.*

*Minialuxe produced some of its miniature cars with friction motors. This Aronde from 1954 and Frégate from 1955 were both issued in 1956. At that time, the Minialuxe range included two other very popular French cars, the Simca Versailles and the Peugeot 403.*

*Anyone who tracks down
this 40 E Standard Vanguard with exposed rear
wheel arches may boast of owning a rare Dinky Toys
model. It was in fact this configuration that was released
in 1948 and 1949. In 1950 the car was marketed as it is
pictured here, with its streamlined rear wheels. It should
be pointed out that the real-life car was also built in
Belgium by Impéria.*

*The 1949 Mercury
saloon was created in miniature
in 1950 by Tekno, who sold it until
1955. A police version also existed,
with the reference number 429.*

*Manufactured in mazac like the vast majority of 1:43-scale models, this Gasqui Septoy is Belgian. This short-lived brand manufactured various models that were interesting, without being of the best quality.*

*Here is the first
model from the German firm Prämeta. It is a Buick 405,
issued in 1952. The original Buick model, known as the
Roadmaster, was the one that brought success to the
firm as it was celebrating its fiftieth anniversary. In fact,
it was David Dunbar Buick, an American of Scottish
origin, like Frank Hornby, who had established the Buick
marque in 1903.*

Another interpretation of the Buick Roadmaster is the wonderful version made by Dinky Toys under reference number 24 V, in February 1954. This miniature in mazac, like all Dinky cars of the time, was manufactured right up to 1959. It was available in several color schemes: orange with a black roof, similar to the one pictured here, as well as yellow with a green roof, blue with an ivory roof, ivory with a metallic blue roof, and lastly, sky blue with a navy blue roof, the most common.

*You could immediately feel the weight and quality
of a Märklin model as soon as you picked it up.
The base of this Mercedes model reveals the imprint
of its transmission system.*

For the most part
Märklin produced only German
cars, with the exception of an Alfa,
one or two Buicks, and Campbell's Bluebird racing car.
This Mercedes 300, Märklin reference number 8003,
was available in a choice of eight different colors.

*Including the Buick*
*on page 56, the four*
*models manufactured by*
*Prämeta are the Jaguar XK 120,*
*the Opel Käpitan, and this*
*Mercedes 300 saloon. They were all*
*released in 1952. Note that Prämeta models were*
*built on a scale of 1:35.*

*Tekno was the maker of this attractive miniature replicating a Mercedes 220.
Observe the Mercedes logo on the radiator cap. This famous three-pointed star
represented the three types of vehicle for which the Stuttgart firm chose to build
engines, those that operated in the air, on land, and at sea.*

Introduced in June 1950,
this 1:43-scale Dinky Toys miniature
is a replica of the 1949 Ford Vedette model.
Its Meccano reference number is 24 Q. It was
a huge success, owing to the 500,000 or more
examples that had been made when the factory
finally closed its doors.

Only six references
for 1:43-scale miniature
cars may be found for GéGé.
In fact, this famous specialist toy
company made various models
on the scale of 1:20.
This self-assembly
Vedette—
it came with a
screwdriver—was
released in 1956.
Its body is
plastic, resting
on a steel
chassis.

*Although the firm of
Mercury dates back to 1932,
it was not before 1945 that it unveiled its first small-scale
model car. Here is the Fiat 600 Multipla, model number 19,
dating from 1957. The forward cab Multipla, based on the
four-cylinder Fiat 600, was a multipurpose version, hence
its name.*

*A Hillman
Minx Series I by Dinky Toys. With
the reference number 175, it was issued in
1958. In actual fact the Minx saloon dates from
before the war and the Series I saloon, with its wide,
low-fitted radiator grille, was in fact the newly
styled version of this extremely popular model that
had been put into production in 1956.*

*This was known as the
Nuova 1100 because it was a
remodeled version of the Fiat 1100 that was beginning to
date after its launch in 1953. So in 1956 the new Nuova
arrived on the scene, whereupon Mercury created a fairly
accurate miniature, with the reference number 13.*

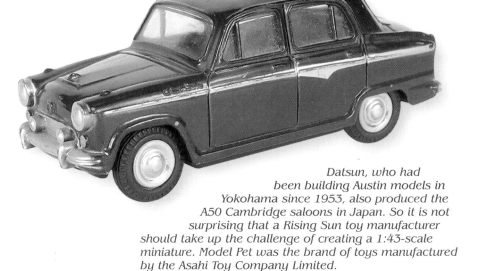

*Datsun, who had been building Austin models in Yokohama since 1953, also produced the A50 Cambridge saloons in Japan. So it is not surprising that a Rising Sun toy manufacturer should take up the challenge of creating a 1:43-scale miniature. Model Pet was the brand of toys manufactured by the Asahi Toy Company Limited.*

*Minialuxe was not
primarily concerned with producing
models that were faithful and accurate
to the originals in shape and size. However,
this Frégate, issued in 1956, a year after the actual
car, does have a certain charm.*

*Although*
this is not obvious from its name,
Mercury was an Italian firm that produced a
variety of Italian cars in the early stages of its career,
followed by a few American cars out of pure fantasy. This Cadillac 62
Sedan illustrates the point perfectly: there is obviously very little
connection between the 5.71-meter-long American model and the 3.24-
meter-long miniature Fiat 500C, which was just then beginning to lose its
popularity in Italy. This Mercury model, reference number 9, was marketed
from 1955 onwards.

When the Régie Renault introduced the
Dauphine, a plethora of colors was made
available with magnificent names such as Pompadour gray,
coral or Montijo red, Butterfly yellow, or Réjane white.
However, when it came to the Dinky Toys version, it seems that this
raspberry red was the only color available. This Renault Dauphine was
made first without windows, then with windows from 1960.

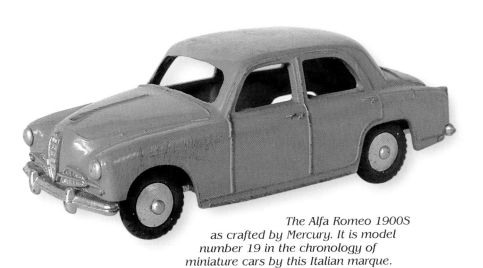

*The Alfa Romeo 1900S
as crafted by Mercury. It is model
number 19 in the chronology of
miniature cars by this Italian marque.*

From June 1962
Dinky Juniors, or the
100 series, appeared.
These attractively priced toys
looked set to conquer a share of the
market, but between 1962 and 1969 only eight models were
marketed under this cheaper label. Here is the Panhard PL17,
reference number 102.

*Built in mazac, this Dyna Z
appeared in the C.I.J. catalogue in 1955, one year
after the unveiling of the real-life car by Paul Panhard.
A red and black G7 taxi version also exists—a very
popular model in Paris since around 1700 of these
vehicles traveled on the capital's streets.*

*The right-hand page shows the front of the Dinky Toys Rover 75, while the reverse is pictured above, far left.*

One astonishing thing about
Dinky Toys is their excellent manufacturing methods.
Illustrated on the left are three chassis, only one of which
shows its axle ends die-cast rather than nipped. The models
seen here are, from left to right, a Rover 75, reference
number 156, introduced in 1954, an Austin Somerset,
reference number 161, introduced onto the market the same
year, and lastly a Singer Gazelle, launched much later in
1959, with the reference number 168.

*The Simca Versailles,
reference number 24 Z, was
marketed by Dinky Toys between 1956 and 1960.
It was a typically French model, designed and
manufactured by Meccano, the chassis of which is
illustrated on page 83.*

The Studebaker Land Cruiser, on the other hand, is a British
Dinky, reference number 172, first released in just one color.
From 1954 it was available in a two-tone color scheme. We
cannot help but be amused by the fact that the two-tone colors
on the box are different from those used for the miniature.

*The Cherryca Phenix
Series were cars manufactured
in Japan between the late 1950s
and early 1960s. No more than
around 50 models, all in mazac, are found in the
catalogues and, as you would expect, the majority are
Japanese cars, including Datsun, Toyopet, Prince, Isuzu,
and Honda. Pictured here is a Dodge Polara, reference
number 10.*

The Lincoln Continental will
take its place in the annals of history as
being the car in which President John
Fitzgerald Kennedy was assassinated in 1963
in Dallas. It was the same model that the Danish company Tekno issued
in 1961. Note that, at the start of the 1960s, the real-life Lincoln was
guaranteed for two years or 24,000 miles.

Lion-Car is a
Dutch brand that created
some exceptional models, including
several Dafs—for patriotic reasons—two
Renaults, one 4CV, and in 1957, a Dauphine. This model is
number LC-105, but it is actually only the ninth model
from this short-lived brand of 1:43-scale cars.

This top-of-the-range model from
De Soto was the Fireflite, which was
equipped with the high-powered 309 horsepower
V8 engine. De Soto, like Plymouth, formed part of
the Chrysler Corporation. Dinky Toys released this
1:43-scale miniature in England in 1958.

*In 1959 the*
*Meccano France catalogue*
*featured the 24 K Simca Chambord*
*with a clear plastic windscreen and windows. Painted in*
*red and ivory or in two tones of green, it was a*
*magnificent example and was the object of envy in every*
*school playground.*

*We should be careful not to confuse the two Simca models, 24 K and 24 Z. The first is the Chambord and the second is the Versailles; the die-cast steel chassis of the latter is pictured here. It was available from Dinky in two color schemes: yellow with a black roof or sky blue with an ivory roof.*

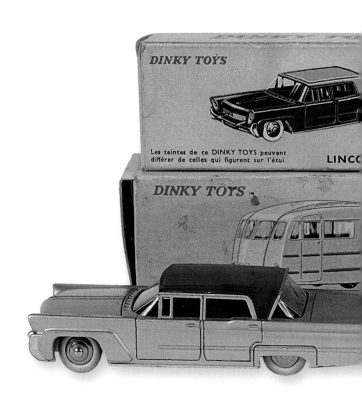

DINKY TOYS

Les teintes de ce DINKY TOYS peuvent
différer de celles qui figurent sur l'étui.

LINCO

DINKY TOYS

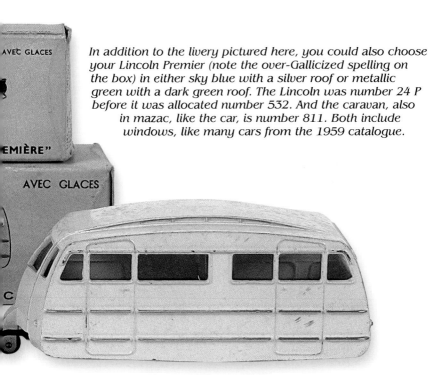

In addition to the livery pictured here, you could also choose your Lincoln Premier (note the over-Gallicized spelling on the box) in either sky blue with a silver roof or metallic green with a dark green roof. The Lincoln was number 24 P before it was allocated number 532. And the caravan, also in mazac, like the car, is number 811. Both include windows, like many cars from the 1959 catalogue.

*Here is a De Soto model,
reference number 545, marketed
by Dinky Toys England from 1959. Notice its
windows and suspension, two brilliant
novelties at the time.*

*After manufacturing
numerous American cars
for export, Dinky Toys England
concentrated on its home market.
This was a worthwhile exercise,
resulting in this Austin Somerset,
reference number 40 J, marketed from
1954 onwards.*

*The Simca 9 Aronde could be found from October 1953 under Dinky Toys reference number 24 U. A taxi version was made available soon after. Production of this model ceased in 1955.*

Also
very popular were the front-
wheel-drive Citroën Traction
Avant saloons, different versions of
which are pictured here, with or without a trunk. The rarest
and therefore the most sought-after models are naturally
those with a spare wheel on the trunk.

*With a single casting of spare wheel and trunk and separate bumpers, this front-wheel-drive Citroën, Dinky reference number 24 N, dates from 1949 and was manufactured with some variations right up to 1959. It has been said that over 500,000 copies of this model had been sold by the mid-1950s.*

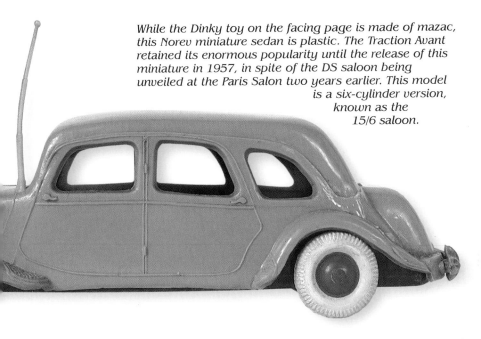

*While the Dinky toy on the facing page is made of mazac,
this Norev miniature sedan is plastic. The Traction Avant
retained its enormous popularity until the release of this
miniature in 1957, in spite of the DS saloon being
unveiled at the Paris Salon two years earlier. This model
is a six-cylinder version,
known as the
15/6 saloon.*

The Citroën 2CV was no different from any other Citroën in that it was
a miniature bestseller for two whole decades. Illustrated here are four Dinky
Toys, with the 24 T version seen from the side, above, and its front view on the
facing page. It was produced from 1952 to 1957 and, when the new numbering

system was introduced in 1959, it became number 535 and could be bought at a price of 200 old francs. On the far right is the 1961 model, the 2CV Azam, which was marketed between 1962 and 1970. It was modified at a later date, when the rectangular headlamps of recent models were fitted.

*The first DS19 created by
Dinky Toys appeared on the market in
November 1956. It had no windows and its reference
number was 24 C, changing to 24 CP when it was
fitted with windows at the Bobigny factory.*

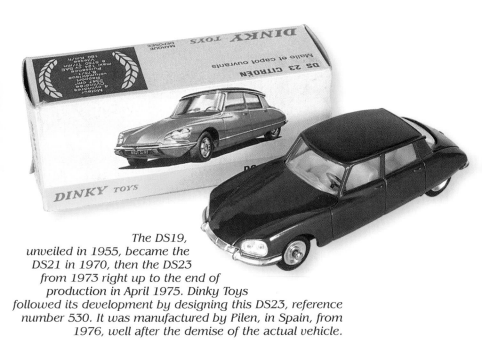

The DS19,
unveiled in 1955, became the
DS21 in 1970, then the DS23
from 1973 right up to the end of
production in April 1975. Dinky Toys
followed its development by designing this DS23, reference
number 530. It was manufactured by Pilen, in Spain, from
1976, well after the demise of the actual vehicle.

*The French Industrial Toy*
*Company, C.I.J., introduced this*
*Frégate Amiral saloon in mazac onto the market in*
*1954. Some models were fitted with clockwork motors. Two-tone*
*Grand Pavois variations were also built from 1958 onward.*

In France,
Belgium, and Switzerland,
Citroëns have always met with great
success. Here is a 1963 Citroën Ami 6 that typified the stunning
work of the celebrated Citroën designer of the moment, Bertoni,
who had already helped in the styling of the 2CV and the DS.

It was pure coincidence
that the camera shot this Politoys Pontiac
Parisienne sports coupé side by side with the
Spot-On Bentley saloon. This latter model, with Spot-On
reference number 102, was released in 1959. Note that
the distinguishing feature of Spot-On models was their
1:42 scale. As far as the Pontiac is concerned, this was
issued in miniature in 1964.

It is well known that the Italian firm Mercury was prolific in its production of Fiat models from different eras. Seen here is a 130 saloon with a 3.2-liter V6 engine. This car was unveiled in the autumn of 1971. Its alloy wheels were designed specially for this model and were reasonably well reproduced by Mercury.

DINKY TOYS

avec direction, suspen-
sion, aménagements
intérieurs et glaces.

OPEL " REKORD "

*The yellow box for this Opel
Rekord, dating from 1960, clearly states that it comes
with steering, suspension, upholstered interior, and
windows. This miniature by Dinky Toys
was marketed from 1961 to 1963.*

*Norev cars were rivals for
Dinky and to some extent Solido. This
Jaguar Mark 1 was issued in 1963 by the French
manufacturer from Villeurbanne and had
the catalogue reference number 24.
A Jaguar Mark 1 may be easily distinguished from
a Mark 11 by its concealed rear wheels.*

*J.R.D. was founded in 1935 but it was not until 1956
that it began to produce 1:43-scale miniature mazac
cars. By the end of 1963, J.R.D. would be sold to C.I.J.
This Peugeot 404 model carries J.R.D. number 151 and
it was first marketed in 1962.*

Nattier blue was the
color Dinky Toys gave this Peugeot
403. Other versions could also be found
in the more serious colors of black, light
gray, and straw, which were better suited to
conventionally middle-class cars. This 403 saloon
without windows was introduced in the 1956
catalogue under the reference number 24 B.

Standing on its own miniature window or counter display unit in lithographed steel is a Chambord saloon, manufactured by Norev with the reference number 40. Issued in 1959 with windows, it was in the standard duo-tone colors of red and cream. Then, from 1963, it received two more possible liveries—blue and pale blue, and an elegant maroon and gray version.

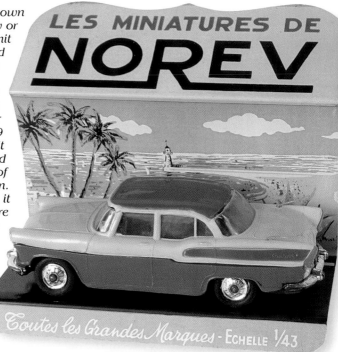

*Created by Solido and reissued soon after for
Hachette, this revolutionary car is the Tucker, one of
only 50 examples built by Preston Tucker in 1947.
Note that this car was ahead of its time with disc
brakes, a steering-wheel-mounted central headlamp,
and other innovations aimed at improving safety.*

*This Peugeot 203 interpreted by Dinky toys is listed*
*as reference number 24 R, which became number 533*
*following the new numbering system, which was*
*introduced in 1959. This Dinky car could be found in a*
*variety of versions and became one of the most widely*
*sold miniatures in France between 1951 and 1959.*

*Eria began production of 1:43-scale mazac models with very popular French cars. This 403 saloon, with reference number 31, was issued in 1958 on a scale of 1:50.*

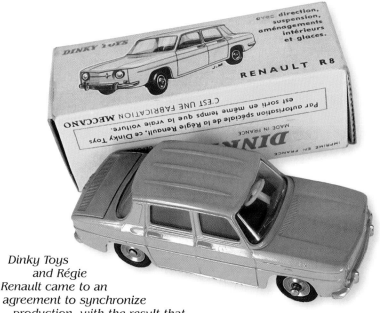

*Dinky Toys
and Régie
Renault came to an
agreement to synchronize
production, with the result that
the real car and its small-scale reproduction
were launched simultaneously onto the market. This was the case for the
launch of the Renault 4 and also the Renault 8, which was marketed, like
the actual vehicle, following the Paris Motor Show in 1962. The only
difference between these two cars was the price, since the real one cost
over a thousand times more than the miniature model.*

The 100 Series
was launched by Solido in 1957. The car manufacturer
from Ivry-la-Bataille in France built this Rolls-Royce Silver Cloud,
reference number 115, between 1960 and 1967. Another color
scheme was available, equally luxurious and chic, in gold and silver.

*This Dinky Toys Peugeot 304, with reference number 1428, was manufactured in France from 1969 to the end of 1971, after which it was produced in Spain up to 1978. The French version is white, while the Spanish one is metallic green.*

*The 1960s and
1970s were periods during which
miniature car factories relocated to Spain
and Portugal. Sometimes companies designed models
specifically geared to their own market, often producing
successful results. This was the case with this Seat 1400C,
created and manufactured by Dalia in the Iberian Peninsula.
Several versions of this model exist, the most notable being
a police car and a taxi. Note that Seat, short for Sociedad
Española de Automóviles de Turismo, was created in 1950
and manufactured Fiats under license.*

**DINKY TOYS**

AVEC GLACES

DINKY TOYS
544
SIMCA "ARONDE"
P. 60
(avec 40 cm)
...

J.M

SIMCA "ARONDE" P. 60

The Simca P60 appeared
on the market at the 1958 Paris Motor
Show. It was in fact a restyled Aronde that was
delightfully updated with a vertical radiator grille and
an altogether glossier surface. The Dinky Toys P60
model was launched a year later and was produced in
the factory at Bobigny until 1963.

ALFA ROMEO GIULIA 1600 TI - Décoration "Rallye"

*The miniature
Alfa Romeo Giulia Ti appeared on the market in 1966.
This car is remembered as being the one in which Andrea de
Adamich made his racing debut. This Dinky model, reference
number 514, was manufactured between 1966 and 1971.*

*Early cars by Politoys, the Italian brand
par excellence, date back to the early 1960s. These 1:43-scale
miniatures aimed at a worldwide audience, which is why numerous
models were created for a huge variety of marques, using the same
casting as this NSU Type 110, a car not often found.*

Politoys in Italy
also produced the Simca
1500, which, like the small-scale NSU on
the facing page, was not very impressive. This concern
with gaining control of the market by producing vast numbers
of cars has left an exciting legacy of diverse models. A special
feature here is the opening hood and the detailed engine.

*The following station
wagons have been included in this
chapter as they are closely related to the
sedan. These wood-bodied station wagons, better known
as Woodies, were very successful in the United States during
the 1950s. Dinky Toys took advantage of this craze by
creating this Plymouth model for the American market.*

*The Belgian
firm Gasqui
Septoy launched this
Jeep Station Wagon at the
end of the 1940s. Although it was similar to the
Plymouth on the facing page in that its body was
made of wood, this was true only for the real-life car.
The small-scale model is in fact made of mazac.*

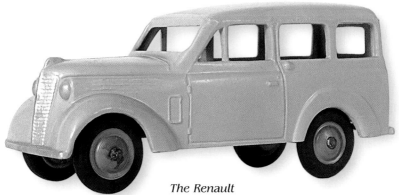

*The Renault*
*Dauphinoise from C.I.J.*
*could be found, like this one, in civilian livery,*
*but a French state police car version also existed.*
*In this case, it was dark blue and equipped with a*
*long radio aerial.*

Lloyd is a small company that was scarcely
known anywhere other than Germany, where it
belonged to Borgward at the beginning of the 1950s.
Tekno no doubt had this market in mind when it
produced this LS 600 station wagon, as well as an
Alexander and a S600 light van. These three models
were introduced in 1958.

*Spot-On cars were manufactured in Belfast, Northern Ireland. from 1959 to 1967, until a fire destroyed the factory. Although this event signaled the demise of this marque, it has nevertheless left a wonderful heritage of some 165 items. The example pictured here is a Land Rover with a long chassis. It is number 161 and was produced from 1962.*

*It was in 1953
that C.I.J., which had strong links
with Renault, put this Colorale model
on the market. It was to have several versions,
one of which was a taxi. The other cars in the
range were the Colorale Prairie and the
Colorale Savane.*

The small
town of Oyonnax in the department of Ain was
once the French capital of the manufacture of plastic.
It is not surprising then that a company should have thought of
producing small-scale models made from this material derived
from oil. Minialuxe manufactured this 203 Peugeot saloon, the
first models of which had no windows. It should be pointed out
that Minialuxe produced mainly French cars during its active
production period between 1954 and 1962.

This Dinky
Junior toy was in the range
from the very beginning. It was
released, as Renault had agreed, at the
same time as the launch of the actual road
vehicle. This Dinky is number 100, the first
of only eight Junior models.

**DINKY TOYS** 193

SPECIAL FEATURES
Fingertip Steering
4-Wheel Suspension
Windows
Seating
Steering Wheel
Plated Fittings

RAMBLER CROSS COUNTRY STATION WAGON

*Aimed above all
at the South African market, the box of this
Rambler Station Wagon lists its special features, including steering,
windows, windscreen, seating, and suspension. This model was
released in 1961.*

*Station wagons were often constructed from the adapted casting of a saloon. This was apparently the case for this Ami 6 Citroen. It appeared in the Solido catalogue from 1965 right up to 1968.*

*The Portuguese
manufacturer Luso Toys was apparently
the only one to produce a Citroen GS
station wagon during the time this vehicle was
actually in production.*

*The experts would say that this Plymouth Sports Suburban station wagon was produced from 1959. They would also add that the early models had a dark gray chassis and that this model was painted a lighter gray from 1960. This just goes to show that the minutest details are invaluable to collectors in the accurate dating of their miniature cars.*

# II

## *Miniature*
# CONVERTIBLES

I f there is one type of automobile body loved by adults and children alike, it is the convertible. The reason it is such a great hit with children is easy to see—they can play with model passengers, putting them in the car and taking them out again to their hearts' content and loading up any back seats with mounds of hurriedly assembled paper luggage.

The word "convertible" is often used interchangeably with the French noun *cabriolet*, which was originally a horse-drawn carriage, deriving from the verb *cabrioler*, to caper or cavort about. Yet this may be the only kind of frolic a car like this cannot perform, equipped as it is with a folding soft top, which in the past was made of leather and nowadays is plastic or canvas. When we think back to the two-wheeled vehicle, we can see just how far the modern cabriolet has come!

*Solido advertising board dating
from the mid-1930s, illustrating
toys that "provide hours of fun."*

*Of course this is a cabriolet,*
but with the system created by Solido in the 1930s, it could also be a
streamlined sedan or an elegant coupé. This Major system, also known
as the 140, manufactured top-quality transformer models that could be
assembled, using bolts, without a great deal of difficulty. They
probably resulted in many collectors entering careers in the automobile
or engineering industries. Both the wheels and bodies were reputed to
be of indestructible metal, unlike the cars made of thin sheet metal,
lead, or papier mâché, which were on the market at the time.

*The famous 100 series that
began at Meccano Limited in 1954 made its first
appearance with this car, a Frazer Nash, so it was
allocated the reference number 100, which may be
seen on its steel chassis.*

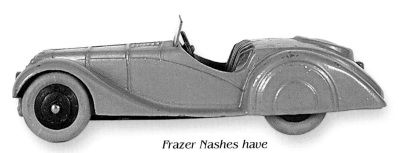

*Frazer Nashes have
always been out and out sports
cars ever since the marque was created in 1924. This model, the
last marque competition car, is in fact a BMW 328, tailored to
British style and built under license in England. This Frazer Nash
was the forerunner of another infinitely more British car in the
Dinky Toys 100 series, the Sunbeam convertible.*

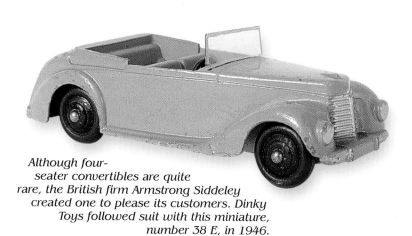

*Although four-
seater convertibles are quite
rare, the British firm Armstrong Siddeley
created one to please its customers. Dinky
Toys followed suit with this miniature,
number 38 E, in 1946.*

Produced by
the French Dinky Toys
factory, this Simca 8 Sport
convertible certainly belongs to the
tradition of British productions. Many
examples of this miniature were issued,
numbered 24 S, between 1952 and 1959.

The Austin-
Healey 100 (the real one,
that is) was a car that was a favorite export
to the United States. Following this trend, Dinky Toys England
created this model, reference 103. As the photo clearly shows,
this is the civilian version with a very smartly dressed driver at
the wheel. This miniature was released in 1957, two years after
the competition version on the facing page.

It is wiser not to put too much faith in the dates used by Dinky Toys and other manufacturers of miniature cars to determine the sequence in which models were launched. Indeed, the Dinky 109 Austin Healey seems to have been released in 1955, two years before the Austin-Healey number 103, which represents just one more mystery in the chronology of this amazing house. The civilian version could be in two different colors, beige or red, and the racing version could be either cream or yellow.

The Triumph TR2 can be distinguished from a TR3 by its recessed front grille. The same trend was true for this car as for the Austin Healey, with the sports version preceding the civilian version. Distributed in 1957, the TR2 touring convertible could be painted either light gray or yellow.

*Magnificently styled like all Dinky cars at the time, this TR2 Sports was marketed from 1956 onwards. In turquoise or sky-blue color schemes, it had number 25 decals on the doors, whereas when it sported a salmon-pink color its number was 29, as this box confirms.*

Contrary to the two cars on the preceding pages, the Aston Martin DB3S, marketed from 1957 with either blue or salmon-pink bodywork, never had a competition version. And yet it was for the most part a racing car, seen in particular at the Le Mans 24 Hours in 1953, to be followed in 1955 by a DB3S finishing second with an average speed of nearly 170 km/h.

*It was in 1959 that Triang, a
famous British toy company,
created the Spot-On brand to market
1:43-scale miniature cars. It was in fact
an attempt to steal a small part of Dinky's
huge market share. It was in 1960 that these right-hand
drive Austin-Healeys were released.*

*With its wide-angled reverse-action motorized hood, this is a Triumph Spitfire produced from 1963. It was very well crafted by Dinky England, except that the girl in the driving seat is sporting a seat belt that is totally out of proportion! What a pity! This Spitfire has the Meccano reference number 114.*

*Here are two MG Midgets
flaunting the only two colors
available for these cars. These
are two competition versions with
drivers in white suits and helmets. The firm MG is so called because
the early marque cars were built by the Morris Garage company.*

*This Austin Atlantic convertible is another very fine example of the Dinky 100 Series in England, marketed from 1954 onwards. Its reference number is 106.*

*This Dinky Toy
was issued in 1947 under
number 38 F, which later became 105.
It is a Jaguar SS 100, although strictly
speaking this is not correct. The truth is
that before the war, William Lyons called
his cars SS after Standard Swallow. With the
return of peace, it was inconceivable to use the label SS for
cars or anything else for that matter. So he chose the jaguar
not only as his crest, but as the name for his factory as well.*

*Until quite recently, around the 1970s, miniature cars sold to children had to resemble the real thing as closely as possible. In a playground it was the done thing to have the latest Dinky, which was generally issued a year after the real car. This Alfa Romeo Zagato from Politoys, which dates from 1967, pioneered the retro look. With reference number 53, modeled on a 1930s Alfa, it marked a real turning point.*

*In 1948 the Jaguar XK120 caused such shock waves following its unveiling at the London Motor Show that numerous toy manufacturers lost no time in making a small-scale model. It was called 120 because it could reach a legendary 120 m.p.h. In 1952 the Danish firm Tekno released the very successful model on the right. Left, a well-known model, the Alfa Romeo, reference number 802.*

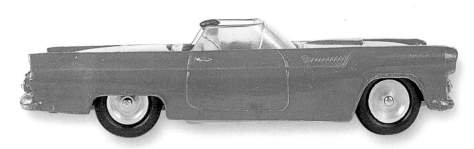

*The Tekno range includes numerous versions of Fords and the Taunus model in particular. Some American Fords have also been very successful, like this 1:43-scale Ford Thunderbird, which was launched in 1959. It is made of mazac and has the reference number 820.*

C.I.J. produced toy
cars in a tremendous
variety of materials. But
after witnessing the success of
Dinky Toys the firm started producing
1:43-scale mazac cars in 1954. Good
choice or bad, this Rovin was their first model
manufactured in this material and on this scale.

*With the splendid number 26 on its door, this is a Sunbeam Alpine convertible, one of the first in the sports car series by Dinky England. In addition to this sky-blue color, this car, reference number 107, might also be painted maroon.*

*This Solido
model, number 133, was produced
from June 1964 to 1969, no month
indicated. It is the Fiat 2300 S Ghia
convertible. Particularly distinctive are the
faceted headlamps, known as jewel
headlights, and the imitation soft top,
simulated with special paint.*

*Three
spectacularly
beautiful American
convertibles, or open-tops, as they
were called then. From left, giving honor
where honor is due, a 1953 Cadillac Eldorado,
reference number 131, released in 1956. Its body,
seating, and dashboard are made from a single
casting, with only the driver added separately. Center,
a Packard, reference number 132, and next to it, a Chrysler New Yorker.
The first two cars are English Dinkys, whereas the third is French.*

*It was surprising
that Dinky did not
include the MGA in its range of toys,
so it was no doubt to fill this gap that Corgi Toys
distributed the first copies of this model in 1957. And, as serious
competitors for Dinky, they obviously intended to cut the ground from
under their feet. The advertising slogan "Collect Corgis" may be seen
on the box flap.*

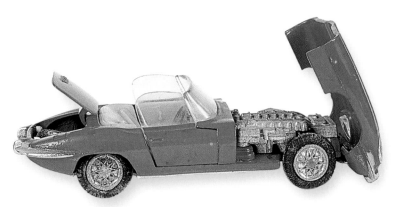

*Made to perfection, this Jaguar E Type incorporates
a working hood that opens to reveal its 6-cylinder
engine. There is also a working trunk and doors.
Various components of this E Type are visible on
the underside, including engine casing, suspension
elements, and muffler. This very realistic creation
was allocated Tekno reference numbers 926 for
the convertible and 927 for the hard-top version.*

*For this Bentley S Series convertible created by Dinky Toys, the drivers were initially cast in mazac and subsequently in plastic. This Dinky model 194 with suspension was released in 1961.*

This Sunbeam
Alpine by Spot-On,
reference number 191, was
delivered with a choice of three
different body tones, white, blue, or green.
It is equipped with suspension, which Spot-On
included as standard on most of its cars from 1961–62
onward. This Sunbeam also existed in a hard-top version.

Henri Chapron was the first to design DS convertibles.
His work was so beautifully constructed that Citroën decided
to order an example to feature in their catalogue, then to
market it throughout their network. Here is an interpretation
of this car by J.R.D., released in 1962. Note that Chapron built
these convertibles in several series of limited editions, using
DS as well as ID chassis.

*Yet another landmark in the history of the automobile is this Alfa Romeo Giulietta convertible, nicknamed the Spider 1300. This miniature, numbered 106, was produced by Solido in their factory at Ivry-La-Bataille, from July 1958 right up to the year 1968. Notice that a woman driver is at the wheel.*

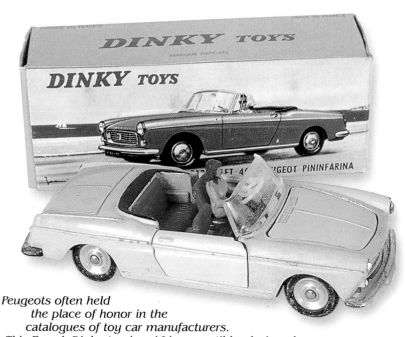

*Peugeots often held the place of honor in the catalogues of toy car manufacturers. This French Dinky toy is a 404 convertible, designed, as everyone knows, by Pininfarina. What is surprising, though, is that this is indicated on the box. This Dinky Peugeot, reference 528, was put on sale from 1965 onwards.*

*Also styled by Pininfarina, this model is a Peugeot 504 convertible, on sale from 1969. This miniature, reference number 1423, included steering.*

It was the Italian stylist Frua who created the lines of the
Renault Floride, the prototype of which was unveiled at the
Geneva Car Show in 1958. It did not enter production before
May of the following year. This is a Solido model, reference
number 109, produced between 1959 and 1965, while the
real car featured in the Renault catalogue only until 1963.

*Another French convertible, the Simca Océane, replaced
the Week-End convertible, which was itself based on the
Simca Sport. Norev managed to release this Océane,
reference number 19, virtually at the same time as the real
car. It is made of plastic, like all Norevs at this time.*

*Yet another Peugeot convertible. Since the 1930s this marque, which in some respects may seem rather old, as indeed it is, has made every effort to produce an open-top version for all its cars, the 402 Eclipse being a typical example. This 204 convertible, Dinky Toys reference number 511, was marketed from 1968 onwards.*

With an all-Italian venture on the cards,
no firm other than Mercury could have produced the Fiat
1500 Spider, particularly when it resulted in such a huge
success. One memorable feature about this model, available
from 1960 in the real-life version and from 1962 in miniature,
was its 1491cc overhead camshaft engine, invented by none
other than the Maserati brothers.

# III

## *Miniatures*
# COUPÉS

In the past a coupé could be distinguished from a conventional two-door car by its maximum number of two side windows, whereas a two-door car could have four, two on each side. What is more, a coupé often implies a sports connection, which is fully justified in many cases.

Nowadays commercial criteria have taken precedence over the true meaning of these terms, and our old standards will soon be nothing more than things of the past. In following this particular trend we have grouped together all two-door cars in this chapter, whether they are sports versions or not. So expect to see a high-performance Aston Martin DB5 next to a humble Volkswagen Beetle, which is closer to a two-door, four-window car than it is to a coupé. But, in the world of toys, what have we to lose?

*The brilliant idea of producing small-scale self-assembly models was the work of Ferdinand de Vazeilles. In mastering the art of pressure die-casting, he pioneered this innovative concept.*

*The Solido cars on these two pages demonstrate how easy it was to swap parts with other models, so that by using the same wheels and chassis, a car could receive different bodies.*

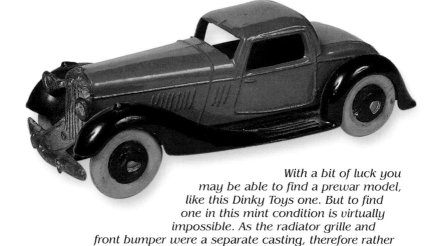

*With a bit of luck you
may be able to find a prewar model,
like this Dinky Toys one. But to find
one in this mint condition is virtually
impossible. As the radiator grille and
front bumper were a separate casting, therefore rather
delicate, it was also the first part likely to break. Note
the rubber tires.*

*If we look more closely at this
Studebaker, we can see that the
paintwork is somewhat rough, proving that it
is perfectly authentic and has never been repainted, which
seems to be quite rare. This model, reference 24 0, has
metal wheels and was manufactured in 1949. The
following year it was made with rubber tires.*

*The Jaguar XK 120 coupés were hugely successful, as much in real life as in miniature. Dinky Toys created this coupé in single and duo color schemes. In 1954 at the Binn's Road Meccano factory in England these cars were allocated reference number 139 D, which became 157 following the new numbering system.*

*A worthy successor to the XK120 and 140, the Jaguar E Type*
*was unveiled at the 1961 Geneva Motor Show.*
*This 1:43-scale model was created by Tekno.*

*Whereas Tekno is a Danish brand, the firm Lion-Car is Dutch. In 1957 it created this miniature DKW Sonderklasse, a small-scale version of the well-known twin-cylinder engine model that carved out a name for itself as one of the most attractive sports coupés in the 1000cc category.*

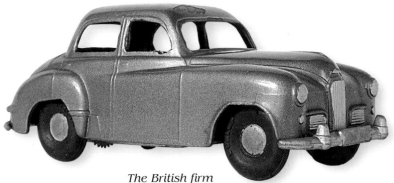

*The British firm*
*Chad-Valley apparently*
*only produced miniature 1:43*
*and 1:60 scale models during 1955. This model is a replica*
*of the Humber Hawk that dates from the early 1950s with*
*its typical three-part grille. We should point out that another*
*Humber, the Super Snipe, was produced by Chad-Valley.*

*The Fiat 1400 was so popular in Italy*
*that Mercury wasted no time in constructing*
*a small-scale model, or rather, several models, since this car*
*was created on different scales. This 1:43-scale car bears the*
*reference number 11.*

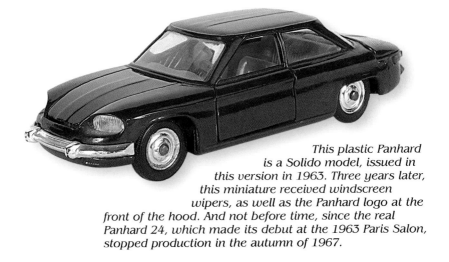

This plastic Panhard
is a Solido model, issued in
this version in 1963. Three years later,
this miniature received windscreen
wipers, as well as the Panhard logo at the
front of the hood. And not before time, since the real
Panhard 24, which made its debut at the 1963 Paris Salon,
stopped production in the autumn of 1967.

*In its Cologne factory in Germany, Ford produced a huge number of cars, among them this 15 M. It was released in miniature in 1956, manufactured by the German firm Märklin. This is the two-door version, reference number 8018. The Taunus 15 M, a very popular car in Germany, was so named for its 1500cc engine that could just reach the maximum speed of 200 mph (125 km/h).*

At a time when the Danish firm Tekno was
producing mainly vans, it also made its name by
manufacturing a quantity of miniature Volkswagens.
Under reference number 819, this coupé appeared in
1959 in four different finishes: civilian, Swiss mail,
and police, with or without a flashing light.

Charming car, charming box. At the time the manufacturing quality of Märklin models could certainly not be faulted in any way. This Volkswagen Karmann Ghia was introduced onto the small-scale model market in 1957, under reference number 8021. We should remember that the lines of this car were styled by Ghia in Turin and the body by Karmann, from Onasbrück, who was responsible for producing it on behalf of VW.

*The Italians at Mercury could not miss out on the Alfa Romeo Giulietta Sprint, designed by Bertone and produced from 1954 to 1963, near Milan. It is said quite correctly that this car represents the birth of the modern Italian sports car. Mercury put this miniature on the market in 1957.*

This
Volvo Amazon, later
named Volvo 120, 121, or 122S,
bears the Tekno reference number 810. This Danish
manufacturer created yet another beautiful Swedish
miniature. Released in 1957 and marketed from 1956 in
the full-size version, it was aimed mainly at the American
market. At the time it was thought to be as great a gamble
as selling fridges to Eskimos!

It was
in 1965 that this
two-door Saab 96 was launched,
with the Tekno reference number 827. It is
said that what distinguishes a beautiful miniature is the
feeling you experience as you hold it in your hand. With
Tekno cars you will never be disappointed: this Saab is so
well finished you will have difficulty putting it down.

*The Opel Rekord 1500 is really quite an unassuming car. Launched in 1956, it was a year later that its 1:43-scale mazac miniature was produced by the Dutch firm Lion-Car.*

The Volkswagen 1500 was released by Tekno in 1962. It was not a great commercial success for either Volkswagen or Tekno, yet it is remarkably well made.

*Although Solido built an
attractive Maserati Ghibly, it was Norev
who created this equally well-made model.
The name of this manufacturing brand from
the Lyon area was formed from an anagram of the
founder's name, Véron. The first Norev cars were
made in plastic, while a series in metal was
introduced at a later date.*

The Maserati 3500 GT, created by the Italian
manufacturer Mercury, was released in 1964.
The sides of the box were illustrated with
drawings as life-like as the Dinky models
of that era.

*This Lancia Flaminia was a representative of top-of-the-range cars with 6-cylinder engines. Mercury copied it in 1960, but Solido also created a model when it had just been put on sale throughout the Lancia network. It was allocated number 121 in the Solido series of miniature cars. Note its lines, styled by Pininfarina in Turin.*

Dalia-Solidos were cars manufactured under license in Spain, or occasionally they were models aimed specifically at the Spanish market. This Alfa Romeo 2600, made in Spain as indicated on the box, enjoyed a long and successful career in France as it did in Spain, where it was produced from March 1963 to the early 1980s.

*Many improvements were brought to the world of the miniature car by Ferrari, with details such as spoked wheels, treaded tires, opening doors, and folding front seats. This car was produced from 1962 to 1968 under reference number 123.*

*Launched in
1967, the Ferrari 275 GTB made
a great impact in its time, in the real-life
version as much as in miniature. The toy
version, with reference number 506, was
produced until 1972.*

*The Lancia Stratos created by Norev appeared in different versions. Released in sports livery for the Monte Carlo Rally, it later became a civilian model, and then reverted to the sports version once more in the Marlboro Texaco colors. The chassis of this debonair coupé, reference number 713, is inscribed with the year of its design, 1972. Other intricate details to note on its bodywork are the HF logo and the emblem of its coachbuilder, Bertone.*

*Clearly visible on the underside
of this De Tomaso Mangusta, created
by Corgi, are its suspension and exhaust.
On the other hand, it has no working features.
The coat of arms belonging to the designer
Ghia is displayed on the hood.*

Number 23 in the new
Mercury series is the coupé
version of the Fiat 2300 S. It
was well crafted, particularly
the rear-window section which
features very slim pillars.

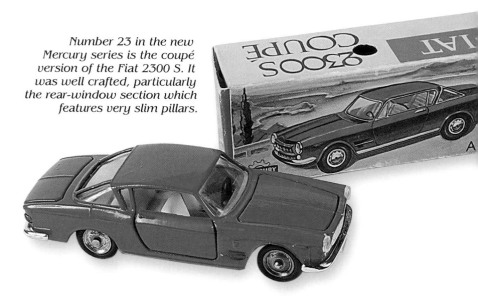

The wheels of this Porsche 356 A are in aluminum. This model must therefore belong to the second series of this stunning replica, as cars from the first series had mazac wheels. It was issued in 1958 with windows and was available in various colors, including this pinkish-maroon, a pale blue, and cream.

CORGI TOYS
304
MERCEDES-BENZ 300SL
HARDTOP ROADSTER

In the history of the Mercedes 300 SL, two models stand out as distinctive: the purest, the coupé with round headlights, and the roadster, with or without hardtop, with rectangular headlights. Both have been attractively styled in miniature. Here are two interpretations of the hardtop roadster issued in 1959 by Corgi (left) and in 1962 by Tekno, reference number 925.

*The firm Quiralu enjoyed its hour of glory during the 1950s, after which it faded into oblivion. An attempt in the early 1990s to reissue some of the old models gave rise to a variety of cars, including this Mercedes 300 SL, released in 1992. The original castings were used for the reissue and the result was an exact match with the first 1956 version, except for the baseplate, which is clearly identifiable on the recent version.*

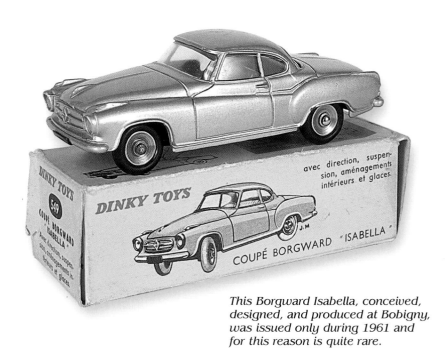

DINKY TOYS

**549**

COUPÉ
BORGWARD
ISABELLA

Avec direction, suspen-
sion, aménagements in-
térieurs et glaces.

avec direction, suspen-
sion, aménagements
intérieurs et glaces.

**DINKY TOYS**

J.M

COUPÉ BORGWARD "ISABELLA"

*This Borgward Isabella, conceived,
designed, and produced at Bobigny,
was issued only during 1961 and
for this reason is quite rare.*

*Although in the past Dinky Toys boxes, almost without exception, were yellow, from 1962 onward they were illustrated with pictures of cars in real-life situations. A case in point was this Mercedes 300 SE coupé (Dinky Toys reference number 533), which was equipped with a windscreen and suspension. It was manufactured from March 1963 right up to 1970.*

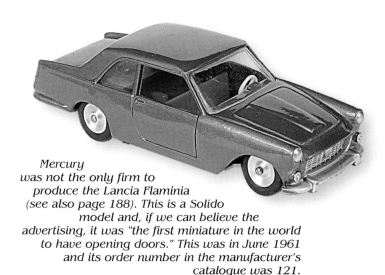

*Mercury
was not the only firm to
produce the Lancia Flaminia
(see also page 188). This is a Solido
model and, if we can believe the
advertising, it was "the first miniature in the world
to have opening doors." This was in June 1961
and its order number in the manufacturer's
catalogue was 121.*

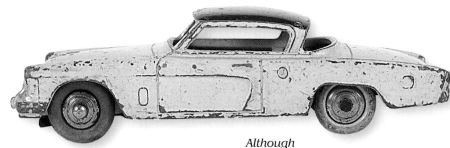

*Although
many miniatures shown in this book
are flawless, earning the description "new and boxed,"
there are some exceptions, notably this Studebaker Commander
with marks that bear testimony to the delight it undoubtedly
gave its owner at the time. It appeared in the 1955 Dinky Toys
catalogue under reference number 24 Y and was also available
in orange with an ivory roof. It was the work of the great
Franco-American designer, Raymond Loewy.*

STUDEBAKER "GOLDEN HAWK"

*Directly derived from the Studebaker on the facing page, this Golden Hawk was issued by Corgi Toys in 1958 under reference number 211. It should be pointed out that number 211M, in addition to the same chassis and body, included a friction motor.*

*The Solido
Ford Thunderbird had
a particularly long career, since it
was produced from May 1963 until at least 1980,
and was also the subject of occasional reissues. Some cars
had painted headlights, while others had jewel headlights,
so called because of their beautiful faceted effect.*

*Cherryca Phenix was a Japanese brand that produced a few models in mazac on a scale close to 1:43. In 1963 it marketed this Ford Thunderbird hardtop, the doors of which were decorated with the Mobil Oil Pegasus decals.*

*Some Dinky Toy cars*
*were manufactured in Hong Kong, which was the case for this 1:42-scale*
*Buick Riviera (reference number 57/000). In addition to this model, seven*
*others were assembled in the independent Chinese city: the Corvair*
*Monza, the Chevrolet Impala, the Dodge Polara, the Oldsmobile Super 88,*
*the Ford Thunderbird, and lastly, the Rambler Station Wagon.*

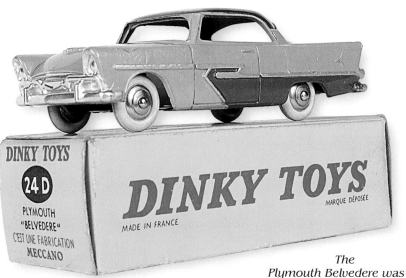

The
Plymouth Belvedere was
assembled in the Meccano factory at
Bobigny from August 1959 to 1961. This model
dates from the period prior to the new numbering
system introduced in 1959, when its reference
number 24 D became 523.

*Worshiped by car enthusiasts, this
Citroen SM with its Maserati engine was,
needless to say, immortalized by Solido
and allocated reference number 184.*

The Renault Floride
was launched as a
convertible as well as a
coupé, and it was this version of
which Dinky Toys created a stunning copy.
This model was produced with windows
from 1960 to 1963.

*The Défense Mondiale was an insurance company that
sponsored Alpine coupé racing cars. This model was created by
Solido who, given the success of the actual car, boosted its
collection by adding not only a rally version but a police version
as well! Note that this coupé is lacking some decals, including
red side stripes and a racing 24 on the doors.*

*Another vast area to explore is that of slot-racing
cars for which Scalextric is the main brand. Here
is a Jouef Alpine with electrical contacts just
protruding beyond the nose.*

This is a 1971 Alpine A310. It was released just about the same time as the actual car, which was unveiled at the Geneva Motor Show in March of the same year. The first version incorporated a 4-cylinder coupé engine, the V6 being introduced only at a later date in 1976. Its Dinky reference number is 1411.

*A miniature Alpine A110
coupé manufactured in plastic
by Norev. It was issued in 1967 as a two-headlight
version, and then in 1970 it received two more, like the
actual vehicle. This is the case in this Norev model,
reference number 59, which has kept intact its original,
delicate, transparent box.*

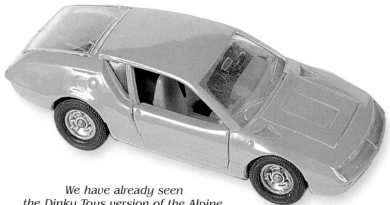

We have already seen
the Dinky Toys version of the Alpine
A310 on page 212. Pictured here is the version
created by Solido, reference number 192, with side
windows that are not as well-made or as accurate as
the real thing. A French state police car also exists as
a variation of this car.

The Lotus Elan S2 roadster may be found in the Corgi range under number 318. The hardtop version is the following reference number 319. This miniature was marketed by the Welsh brand from 1965 onward. Note that the Lotus Elan was Jim Clark's personal car.

*These
exquisite creations
seem to be the first "closed" models
produced by Solido in the twentieth
century. In fact, until this time, Solido
had only produced racing cars or convertibles. Here are
two versions of the Aston Martin DB4, which was
produced from autumn 1960 up to 1965.*

Since the DB4 was fashionable at the time, nearly all manufacturers followed suit with their own small-scale version. At the same time as Solido, Corgi issued this Aston Martin under number 218, but unlike the Solido model, theirs had a hood that opened.

Corgi adopted
opportunistic strategies that allowed them
to survive longer than other firms. For example, it made a clever
move in buying the rights to certain films, producing vehicles used
by Spiderman and other film heroes. By 1965 the James Bond Aston
Martin DB5 was marketed under reference number 261.

*No one could deny that James Bond's car was a collector's dream, with its ejector seats, retractable machine guns, and rear bulletproof screen. The miniature Corgi copied all these gadgets, with the added bonus of a "secret instructions" leaflet. As for the box that could also be used to display the car, this too gave food for thought.*

It is a pity, but it must be said that miniature cars no longer continued to be accurate and faithful copies of the originals when toy manufacturers decided to fit opening doors, working hoods, suspension, and steering. In other words, it was too much all at once, and this signaled the beginning of the end. Here is an Opel Rekord 1900 coupé that was produced from 1968 to 1970, under reference number 1405.

For a while,
Norev used the same models
to synchronize production of
plastic and mazac miniature cars. It seems that
this Renault benefited from the two versions
during the period 1972 to 1979.

*This 1955 Lancia Aurelia B20 was an ace rally car in its time, in the same way as the Fulvia and the Stratos would be at a later stage. Norev recognized the trend and included this model in its range from 1958.*

*It was in 1966 that Politoys issued the Lancia Fulvia in mazac. This Italian brand, which manufactured miniature cars in plastic, had already produced this Fulvia in 1964 in this far less impressive material.*

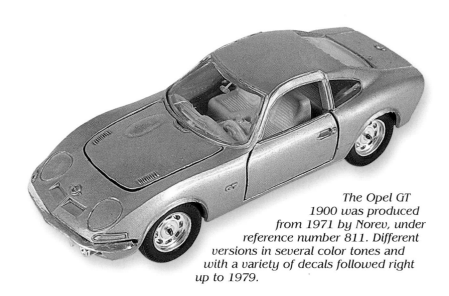

*The Opel GT 1900 was produced from 1971 by Norev, under reference number 811. Different versions in several color tones and with a variety of decals followed right up to 1979.*

*The triumphant exploits of Facel Véga, the brainchild of Jean
Daninos, came to an end with this model that strangely
enough turned out to be the most popular of all. By all
accounts it was the firm C.I.J. who created this 1961 copy
on a scale of 1:43, reference number 3.3.*

*Less famous than the Alpine coupé, the
Matra Djet, invented by René Bonnet, was
a captivating car, built in Romorantin.
Pictured here is the Minialuxe version.*

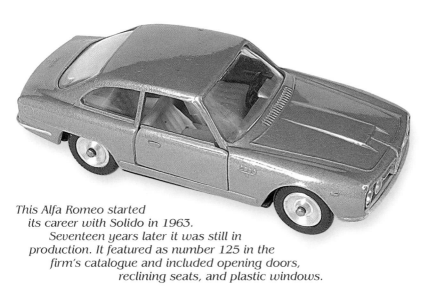

*This Alfa Romeo started
its career with Solido in 1963.
Seventeen years later it was still in
production. It featured as number 125 in the
firm's catalogue and included opening doors,
reclining seats, and plastic windows.*

According to the experts this was a
well-styled Ford Mustang
from 1966 that was
issued the following
year by Tekno and
was marketed
for three years
under reference
number 834.

Originally it was the coachbuilder Frua who designed this 3.5-liter Maserati. Solido in its turn created a version in 1965. In fact, this turned out to be the first model in the new "Haute Fidélité" range by this manufacturer of miniature cars.

*This Fiat revolutionized Italy in the mid-1930s. There it was known as Topolino, Micky Mouse in Italian! This is one of the first all-French Dinky Toys models, a replica of the Simca 5, which was the French-manufactured Fiat.*

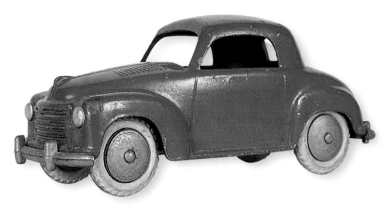

*Like the Fiat on the facing page, this one is in mazac.*
*But whereas the first—Dinky Toys 35 A from 1939—*
*has no chassis, this model, manufactured by*
*Mercury, does include one.*

The Vespa 400 was a French creation that borrowed the engine and certain components from the Italian Vespa. They were manufactured in the Vespa ACMA factory at Fourchambault. This miniature, number 24l, was launched by Dinky Toys at a price of 340 francs in 1959. It was made in blue but also exists in orange, which is much rarer. It was produced right up to 1963.

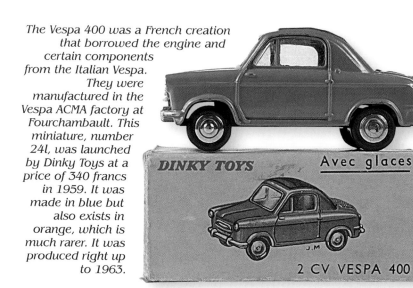

In spite of its British-sounding name, Midget Toys is undoubtedly a French brand. Apart from this Vespa 400, it produced a Vanwall, a Jaguar, a Dyna Panhard, and a Citroën DS19, all apparently in 1959.

Small Dafs manufactured
in Holland belong to one of the rare car marques
found in this flat country. Why else did Dinky Toys
decide to produce one of its models, the smallest
in fact, if it was not with this particular market in
mind? Note the figure of a plastic lady at the wheel
of this car, numbered 508 and produced between
1966 and 1971.

*It was the Italian firm Mebetoys who issued this Fiat 500. They produced 1:43-scale cars in mazac from 1966 and their catalogue included mainly Italian cars.*

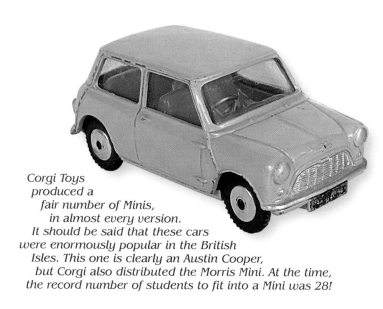

Corgi Toys
produced a
fair number of Minis,
in almost every version.
It should be said that these cars
were enormously popular in the British
Isles. This one is clearly an Austin Cooper,
but Corgi also distributed the Morris Mini. At the time,
the record number of students to fit into a Mini was 28!

*We
surely need
no reminding that
it was Alec Issigonis who designed the
Mini, having the clever idea of setting the
engine transversely instead of longitudinally,
so as to reduce the overall length—an idea that was to
catch on throughout the world. This English Dinky Toys
model replicates the estate version, which has the same
dimensions as the Countryman estate.*

It was Lion Car,
a company specializing
in miniature cars in Holland, that
produced this Daf 55 coupé. The other Dutch
miniature car brand was Best Box, which also
manufactured cars in mazac, but only had foreign cars
in its collection.

*Even the Fiat 500, a very small car modestly powered by
its twin-cylinder engine, was entitled to its estate version,
known in Italy as Giardiniera. Politoys made this marvelous
miniature car that was extremely successful in Europe.
That goes for the real car as much as its miniature model.*

*In the 1980s the Japanese
started a revival of the lines that were
popular in the 1950s. Nissan launched this
car, labeled PAO, for which Diapet de Yonezawa created
a 1:40-scale version in the Minicar Collection.*

*Unveiled
in 1959, the Mini celebrated its
thirtieth anniversary in 1989, and only
a few journalists were presented with a
Corgi Toys gift set comprising this miniature
model and a book recounting its real success
story. Its base is inscribed "Mini 30 1989,"
and its 1:36 scale is also indicated*

# IV

## *Miniature*
# RACING CARS

Children loved to bring their racing cars to school playgrounds where they could find a sheltered area and . . . race them. Of course, no child would ever have thought of bringing along a van as a match for a Talbot, a Ferrari, or an HWM. Identical in concept to real Formula 1 cars and encapsulating their finest attributes, these small-scale models were cut out for racing, better than any other miniature car. Generations of school children have enjoyed these games and in doing so have learned the names of marques and drivers, as well as international racing colors, by reciting them out loud: Italian red, French blue, Belgian yellow, German gray, and British racing green. What music to their fanatical ears!

*In 1933 the media
repercussions surrounding the
records achieved by this Citroën "Petite Rosalie" were
immense. Piloted by César Marchand and his team, this car began its marathon
on March 15 and completed it on July 27, 137 days and almost 200,000 miles
(300,000 km) later! And that was at an average speed of 60 mph (93 km/h),
including all stops. So it is not surprising then that this Citroën, which was
awarded a total of 106 world records as well as 191 other class and category
records, was replicated in a variety of versions. This one, made from plaster and
flour, is the work of C.I.J., who manufactured Citroën toys*

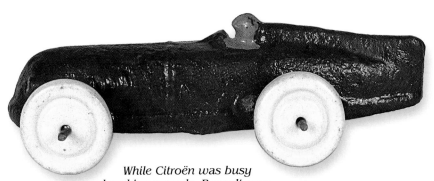

*While Citroën was busy
breaking records, Renault was
also getting in on the act. In fact, it was Louis
Renault who started this contest in the mid-1920s
with his 40CV models. The car pictured here, of no
known brand, is made of a type of terracotta and
its scale is close to 1:50.*

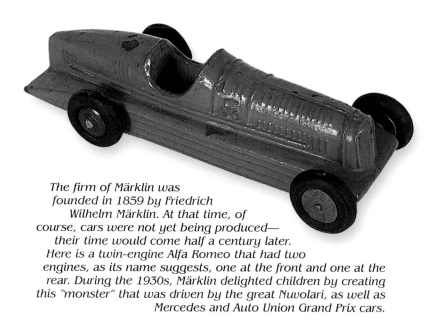

The firm of Märklin was
founded in 1859 by Friedrich
Wilhelm Märklin. At that time, of
course, cars were not yet being produced—
their time would come half a century later.
Here is a twin-engine Alfa Romeo that had two
engines, as its name suggests, one at the front and one at the
rear. During the 1930s, Märklin delighted children by creating
this "monster" that was driven by the great Nuvolari, as well as
Mercedes and Auto Union Grand Prix cars.

*It is a well-known fact that Renault took over from Citroën
as the major name in toy cars, giving rise to this record-
breaking 28CV Nervasport. Made of plaster and flour, this
somewhat delicate toy was manufactured by C.I.J. between
1935 and the late 1940s, which goes to show the impact
of three world records (the 4,000 and 5,000 miles and the
48 hours), established between April 3 and April 5 1934,
at an average speed of over 100 mph (167 km/h).*

*Jep toys were enchanting cars in silk-screen-printed sheet metal, bearing little resemblance to the real thing. Although Jep is known for its superb large toys, the firm also produced these miniature cars, which allowed children to play their games on a table, unlike the big Jep cars that were more suited to a concrete kitchen floor.*

*Jouets de Paris, or Jep as it is commonly known, featured the Delage and Bugatti models in their catalogue, reference numbers 675 and 676 respectively. These could also be fitted with clockwork motors, in which case they were allocated reference numbers 7675 and 7676.*

*This
attractive racing car, inspired by
a 1939 Maserati, was one of the first
miniatures in plaster and flour from J.R.D. This
car, like the majority of toys at the time, was not
packaged individually, but was delivered as one of a box
of six that were sold singly by the retailer.*

*With racing number 2
stenciled on its side, this
charismatic MG Magic Midget was
one of the first Dinky Toys created by Meccano
in England. It was first issued in lead in 1935, then later in
mazac. It was marketed right up to the late 1940s. Do not
forget that with Eyston in the cockpit, this 750cc MG broke
the 120 mph speed record in 1932.*

*It is not surprising to learn that early models took their inspiration from performance racing cars. These were certainly very popular between the two world wars. The Brooklands and Montlhéry circuits, not to mention several emerging freeways, witnessed ruthless battles for record-breaking victories. Here, under Dinky Toys reference number 23 B, is a Hotchkiss, which was manufactured in 1935 and reappeared in the catalogue after the war.*

*This Dinky Toys racing car measuring 4 inches (10.5 cm), reference number 23 E, is nicknamed "Speed of the Wind." It is found in the catalogue of 1938–39, where it is mentioned as "a former holder of world records."*

*This record-breaking
Auto Union was a prewar
production by Dinky Toys in
England. On February 15 1935, this quite spectacularly
streamlined racer broke the speed record of 200 mph (320
km/h) piloted by Hans Stuck on the Florence freeway. Only
two years later and under the same conditions, another
Auto Union broke the 200 mph barrier!*

George Eyston
was one of the pioneers who
risked their lives and possessions in the
quest to beat yet another record. His Thunderbolt
of nearly 5000 horsepower "achieved 326 mph,"
(575 km/h) claimed the Dinky Toys catalogue of
1938–39, in which it featured as reference
number 23 S.

*The Talbot Lago
is the racing car par excellence. In
addition to this single-seater, its 4.5-liter
engine also furnished sports cars and luxury
touring cars. Small children considered it
their prize weapon in the school playground.
One feature they could never forget was its huge rubber
tires jutting out beyond the radiator grille, allowing it to bounce off
any wall it encountered and set off again in reverse at the same
speed. Its Dinky Toys reference number is 23 H and it was
marketed from 1953.*

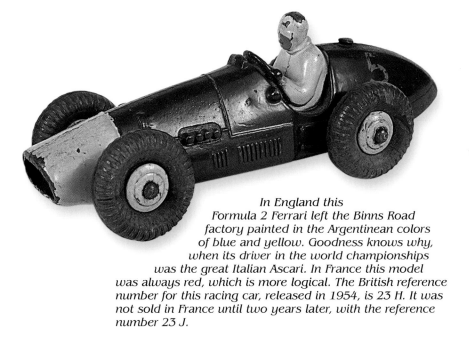

In England this
Formula 2 Ferrari left the Binns Road
factory painted in the Argentinean colors
of blue and yellow. Goodness knows why,
when its driver in the world championships
was the great Italian Ascari. In France this model
was always red, which is more logical. The British reference
number for this racing car, released in 1954, is 23 H. It was
not sold in France until two years later, with the reference
number 23 J.

*This Dinky Toys car
bears the reference
number 23 J under the old
system, changing to 235 when the new
numbering came into effect. Launched in 1953, it is worth
noting that the body and driver were molded in a single casting.
This model was renowned for introducing the small marque
HWM to children who only swore by Talbot, Ferrari, or Maserati.
In case you do not know, HWM stands for Hersham and Walton
Motors and its director was John Heath.*

*It was in a Cooper Bristol
racing car similar to the one
pictured here that Mike Hawthorn
made his debut during the 1952 Formula 1 season.
This event merited his taking the wheel in a Ferrari the following
year. Several years later, Cooper would reverse the driver-engine
position by fitting the engine in the rear. This Dinky 23 G Cooper
was in production from 1953 to 1964.*

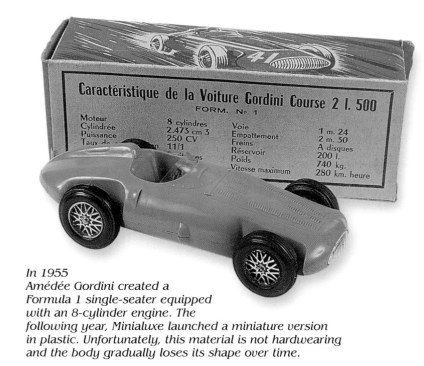

Caractéristique de la Voiture Gordini Course 2 l. 500
FORM. N° 1

| Moteur | 8 cylindres | Voie | 1 m. 24 |
| Cylindrée | 2.473 cm 3 | Empattement | 2 m. 30 |
| Puissance | 250 CV | Freins | A disques |
| Taux de | 11/1 | Réservoir | 200 l. |
| | | Poids | 740 kg. |
| | | Vitesse maximum | 280 km. heure |

*In 1955*
*Amédée Gordini created a*
*Formula 1 single-seater equipped*
*with an 8-cylinder engine. The*
*following year, Minialuxe launched a miniature version*
*in plastic. Unfortunately, this material is not hardwearing*
*and the body gradually loses its shape over time.*

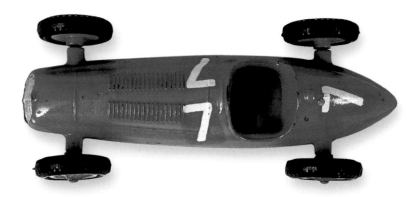

*Whether it was just timely or well planned, the release of this Maserati in 1957 coincided with Fangio's victory in the world championship with this Trident of Bologna. It was surely the least Mercury could do, given that it was an Italian toy firm— although you would never guess that from its name! With the reference number 34, this model apparently never had a driver at the wheel.*

The Maserati 250F is
one of the sacred monsters of
the racetrack. The British firm Crescent
Toys was well aware of this when they introduced this single-seater,
reference number 1290, onto the market from 1957. It could not
have been released at a more suitable time, since it was the year
that Juan Manuel Fangio won his fifth and last world championship
title in a Maserati 250F. It was not exactly this version, but that was
of little importance to little boys and girls who were only too
pleased to show off this car to their classmates—after all, it was the
car piloted by the great "El Chueco!"

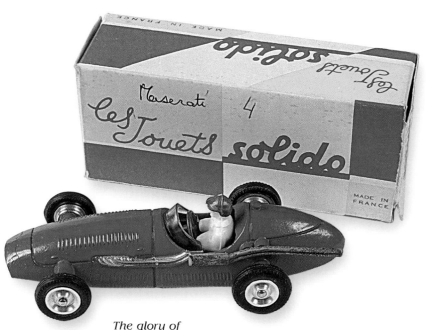

The glory of
Maserati must certainly have
been great in view of the fact that Solido produced this other
version of the 250F, between the month of December 1957—since
this topic calls for absolute precision—and 1965. Rear-engine cars
had long taken the place of front-engine vehicles. This Solido racer
features in the catalogue under the reference number 102.

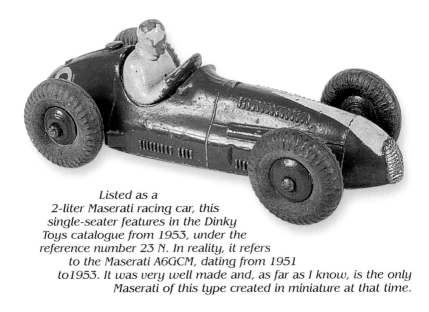

Listed as a
2-liter Maserati racing car, this
single-seater features in the Dinky
Toys catalogue from 1953, under the
reference number 23 N. In reality, it refers
to the Maserati A6GCM, dating from 1951
to1953. It was very well made and, as far as I know, is the only
Maserati of this type created in miniature at that time.

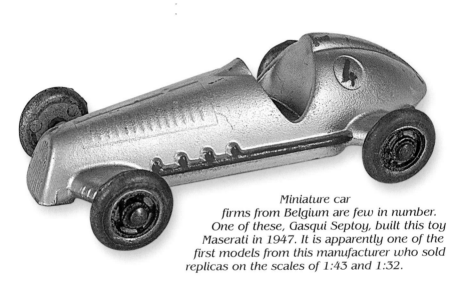

*Miniature car
firms from Belgium are few in number.
One of these, Gasqui Septoy, built this toy
Maserati in 1947. It is apparently one of the
first models from this manufacturer who sold
replicas on the scales of 1:43 and 1:32.*

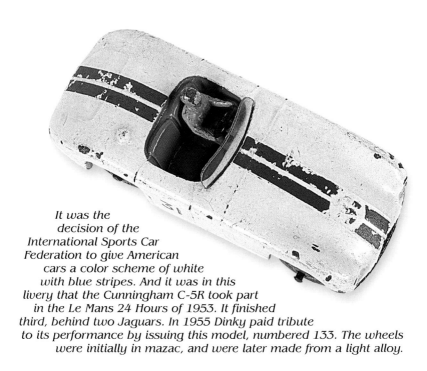

It was the
decision of the
International Sports Car
Federation to give American
cars a color scheme of white
with blue stripes. And it was in this
livery that the Cunningham C-5R took part
in the Le Mans 24 Hours of 1953. It finished
third, behind two Jaguars. In 1955 Dinky paid tribute
to its performance by issuing this model, numbered 133. The wheels
were initially in mazac, and were later made from a light alloy.

*One of
Solido's bestsellers
was unquestionably this Jaguar
D-Type, produced right up to 1971. It was
the first in the Solido 100 series, at a time when
the actual racer had just achieved another glorious victory
at the Le Mans 24 Hours of 1957. That year the Flockhart-Bueb team
was triumphant, finishing ahead of three other Jaguar D-Types. It
should be pointed out that this miniature has suspension, and the
3442cc capacity of the real model is indicated on the box.*

*These fantastic aerodynamic lines belong to the Bristol 450 racing cars that lined up at Le Mans in 1953 and 1954. In their second qualifying year, they finished seventh, eighth, and ninth in the overall standing. In the light of this success Dinky Toys issued this miniature the following year, under the reference number 163.*

*If Ferrari is now the most celebrated name in world racing cars, Maseratis were equally well known throughout the 1950s because of their prewar achievements. This accounts for the quantity of miniatures bearing the Trident marque. Here is a Maserati 2-liter A6GCS released in 1958 with the Dinky Toys reference number 22 A.*

This car
was known
as the Maserati
200S. It was a 2-liter
4-cylinder "barchetta" model,
of which 28 examples were produced from
1955. Thankfully, Norev issued a much greater number of copies,
accounting for its frequent appearance in school playgrounds.
With Norev reference number 20, it was marketed in 1958 and
its racing numbers range from 1 to 9.

This Ferrari Testa Rossa was created by Solido in 1958. Its realism was marred by its dashboard—at least on the early models—which was in green plastic, not a classic English green, but an unrealistic apple-green! This car was produced until 1965, the date of the last victory for this marque in the Le Mans 24 Hours.

It was
on the salt lake
at Bonneville in the state of
Utah that the Etoile Filante, piloted
by Jean Hébert, took the world speed record
for turbine-powered cars. The speed of 190 mph (309
km/h) seems quite modest by modern standards, but we are
talking here about the year 1956. The car's engine was a
270bhp Turbomeca, generally used in aeronautics. The
miniature version is by Quiralu.

This car that
conquered every circuit
in the world, as well as coastal and
rally tracks, is even more renowned for being
James Dean's car, at the wheel of which he met his death
at Salinas in 1955. Manufactured by Solido from 1957 to
1965, this Porsche Spyder 550/1500 RS was allocated the
reference number 101.

This amazing Alfa Romeo received notorious acclaim
for earning Nino Farina the world driving championship
title in 1950 and Juan Manuel Fangio the following
year. This miniature gives a very realistic portrayal of
the amount of machinery required to equip these huge
front-engine Formula 1 cars. The tail fin functioned as
the fuel tank. It is a Dinky Toys model, reference
number 23 F, marketed from 1954 onward.

*Two incredible British men, Charles and John Cooper, realized well before anyone else that Formula 1 cars could be small and light. And in spite of being less powerful, they could still win races. This rear-engine 1500cc Cooper—Solido number 116 from 1960—illustrated this well, achieving world champion racing car status in 1959 and 1960 with Jack Brabham at the wheel. So, for F1 it was the definitive break with front-engine single-seaters—at least, that is the situation today, but we never know what tomorrow will bring.*

Its "SGDG patented
suspension," which was
inscribed on the chassis, was real progress for the
period. By including this detail, Solido made their miniatures
even more realistic. This British, front-engine, single-seater
Vanwall was led to victory by Stirling Moss. A hero of the 1950s
and victorious in numerous Grand Prix races, he was never
world champion. From 1955 to 1961, Moss, the "champion
without a crown," was four times second and three times third
in the championships

*The cars
participating in the Indianapolis 500 Miles
were exceptional, of very different designs
to European Formula 1 cars. This turbine-
powered STP racing car, with its offset
cockpit, was created in France in 1969
under American license by Faracars.*

It was following the
performance-rated Cornet-
Cotton victory at the Le Mans 24
Hours of 1959, in a Panhard DB HBR4, that
this miniature was put into production. It was a
stroke of luck that on its release the following year, another
almost identical DB was again victorious at Le Mans. The racing "46"
might be realistic, but the tricolor strip on the hood is certainly not.

Of these
two cars sold as
racing car miniatures,
only the Alfa Romeo GTZ,
front, had a real sports career
by participating in circuit races and rallies. The
Corvair Monza at the back was more of a show car, spectacular
yes, but with no sports victories to its name. The Alfa Romeo GTZ is a Solido,
reference number 148; the Corvair Monza is a Tekno, reference number 930.

At a time when Dinky Toys was still selling its front-engine
Formula 1 cars, Solido, by 1960, was issuing its very
realistic miniature Cooper. Dinky Toys took until 1963 to
respond with this Cooper-Climax for small boys who had
a craving for up-to-the-minute models. It has a working
hood made in plastic and is numbered 240.

*When Dinky Toys revamped its
Formula 1 range in 1963, the series, although not
complete, comprised this Ferrari, the Cooper on the opposite
page, a BRM, and a Lotus, all Formula 1 single-seaters
requiring 1500cc engines in line with new racing regulations.*

*Keeping ahead of
current trends has always been an ambition
for manufacturers of miniature cars. That is why Dinky Toys created
this Ferrari, identical to the one driven by Jacky Ickx when he won
the Grand Prix de l'ACF in July 1968 on the circuit at Rouen-Les-
Essarts. Out of their concern for details and prices, Dinky Toys
included plastic components such as the engine, driver, and wings,
thus making their cars less sturdy.*

With the arrival of advertising for Formula 1 in particular and sports car racing in general, manufacturers of miniature cars came up with the idea of enclosing decals in the boxes. It was then up to the children to stick them on the cars, which gave many of them their first steps in model-making. Depicted here is the Surtees F1 of 1969, Dinky number 1433.

The French were especially happy to find this Formula 1 Matra in their favorite shop, not only because of its very realistic 12-cylinder engine but also because its driver, Jean-Pierre Beltoise, was the inspiration behind the revival of sports car racing in France—two good reasons for buying this Dinky Toys car numbered 1417, which was released in 1969.

*With its "spaghetti"
exhaust pipes and realistic
wheels, the Ferrari V12 from
Solido looked amazingly authentic. It was the car of
the 1967 racing season, which holds sad memories
for the Scuderia team who witnessed the fatal
accident of Lorenzo Bandini in Monaco. The model
was released by Solido in 1968 and was
manufactured until 1971.*

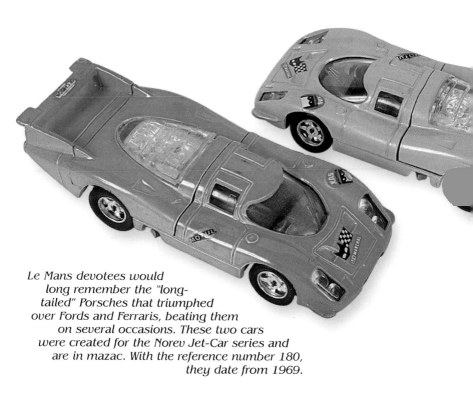

*Le Mans devotees would long remember the "long-tailed" Porsches that triumphed over Fords and Ferraris, beating them on several occasions. These two cars were created for the Norev Jet-Car series and are in mazac. With the reference number 180, they date from 1969.*

*Here is another Solido interpretation of the Porsche 917, distinguishable from those on the facing page by its "short tail." The Stuttgart firm used this version for rugged circuits where reaching top speeds was not really crucial.*

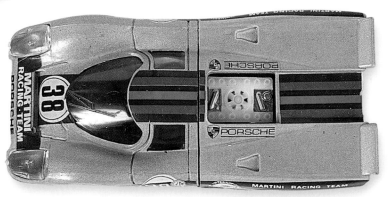

*These 1:66-scale cars were manufactured by Safir Champion and marketed in the early 1970s*

*French miniature racing cars were rare. When this modest French blue Alpine Formula 3 was introduced onto the market, it filled a gap for enthusiasts. Nevertheless, it was not spectacular enough to really catch on. This single-seater was piloted by François Cevert for its debut race and was manufactured by Solido under reference number 142 from 1965 to 1969.*

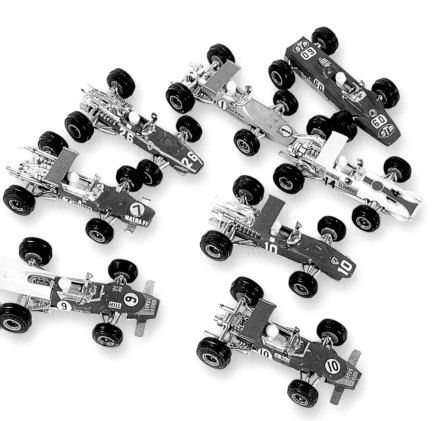

*The chassis of this car is inscribed with "Ferrari Berlinetta 250 Le Mans, patent no. 904525, made in Great Britain."*
*Very well crafted by Corgi Toys, this car that won the Le Mans 24 Hours in 1965 was issued the same year, which made it an immediate success.*

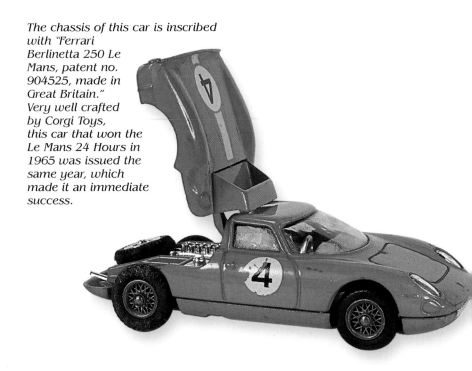

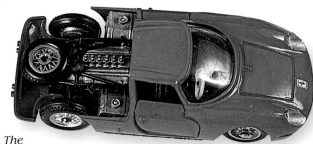

The
Italian firm
Mercury also created a Ferrari 250LM.
Like the Corgi version, its rear hood opened to reveal
its engine but, what's more, on this model, the hood could be taken off
completely. On the subject of the real 250LM, it must be remembered that
Enzo Ferrari wanted this car to be authorized as a vehicle to be used on
the road, like the GTO, but the international motor sport authorities
declined his request.

You would have to be Italian to replicate an Abarth model. And the Italian firm Mercury, of which we need no reminder, did precisely that. It brought out at least two models, the 1000 Bialbero coupé and the 1000 OT. The first of these, pictured here, was victorious on circuits and rallies and was particularly renowned for canonizing the driver Franco Patria. He was to meet his death at the Paris 1000 kilometers in 1964, in the cockpit of one of these racers. Let us not forget that in this drama three track stewards also lost their lives, as did Peter Lindner, who was driving a Jaguar E Lightweight.

*Dated 1973 on*
*its chassis, the real-life model of*
*this Chevron B23 had a 2-liter engine*
*and participated in the hotly disputed*
*European championships. Its metal replica was*
*extremely well crafted by Norev, reference number 834.*

*The firm of Chaparral was founded in the mid-1970s by Jim Hall and Hap Sharp. They were two Texans who wanted to put into practice their revolutionary ideas on competition racing. Here is a Chaparral 2J created in Italy by Mercury, reference number 310.*

It was this type of replica, well constructed, but with
unconventional wheels (that could be found on all kinds of
different models), which was the reason for aficionados of
miniatures moving away from the bigger manufacturers to
favor smaller craftsmen. These put more care and precision
into their models and details such as wheels were not
overlooked.

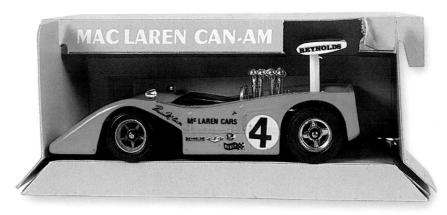

*Is it the memory of Bruce McLaren at the wheel that makes this McLaren M8B CanAm appear so stunning in its orange livery? The CanAm races, which took place between the United States and Canada, saw beasts of extraordinary power pitted against monsters blazing with brightly colored stickers. With Solido reference number 176, this car has a chassis dated March 1970. This was the year when Bruce was killed at Goodwood, at the wheel of one of his cars.*

*The late 1970s saw enthusiasts for miniature toys make a fairly sudden transition to models that were authentic and extremely professional.*

*This one in resin is a replica of the Ferrari 330P driven by Jo Bonnier and Graham Hill at the Le Mans 24 Hours event of 1964. It was created by Jean-Pierre Viranet, who signs his productions with an anagram of his name, Tenariv.*

# V

*Miniature Working*
# VEHICLES

There are cars intended for everyday driving and there are those designed for work, a tremendous variety of which may be found in all shapes and sizes: solemn black cars enveloped in their flags, immaculate white vehicles with beautiful red crosses, as well as those with permission to ignore traffic lights, modest delivery vans, and taxis. And then there are also cars displaying the labels of Her Majesty's coat of arms, Swiss mail, mountain rescue, or the Royal Air Force. And let's not forget military vehicles! How wonderful to be part of this khaki-colored universe at an age when innocence reigns supreme. All these official cars or commercial vans must certainly have set many a child on the road to a career for life. And manufacturers of miniature toys could not have had an easier task than launching a magnificent new creation by revamping a civilian car that had served its time.

*This very rare municipal
ambulance in lead by the brand CD may be
dated to 1931 or 1932. This marque (which should
not be confused with DC, another French firm in operation
before the Second World War) is very old, its origins dating
back to 1925. This toy represents a Delahaye van that
carried a small Red Cross flag, which is absent here.*

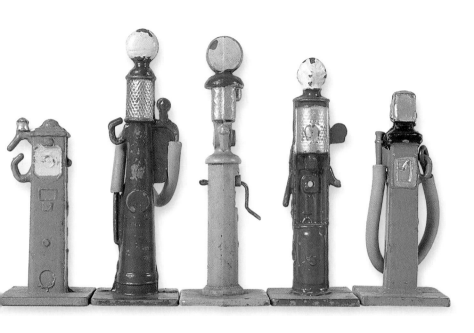

*All these petrol pumps are English Dinky Toys, except the one in the center, which is also by Dinky but is a French model. Each is more charming than the next, even though the hoses may sometimes be missing.*

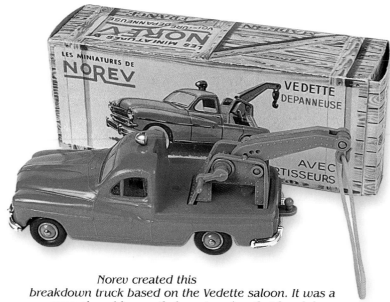

*Norev created this
breakdown truck based on the Vedette saloon. It was a
marvelous idea on their part seeing that breakdown
vehicles did not exist in huge numbers. Released in 1960,
this Vedette 1954 was allocated the reference number 34. Three
variations of this model apparently existed between this date and 1963.*

*Dinky Toys*
*converted the renowned Citroën U-23 lorry*
*into a breakdown truck, reference number 35.*
*With the introduction of the new numbering system*
*in 1959, it was to become 582. This bestseller was*
*produced from 1955 to 1971. On the model pictured here, the metal*
*hoist that was activated by the tiny chrome handle is missing.*

*It is not a coincidence that Corgi sounds similar to Dinky. In fact Mettoy, a specialist toy company since 1933, started producing cars in 1948, but it was only in 1956 that the first Corgi Toys appeared. It seems that this name was chosen not only to create a certain amount of confusion with Dinky Toys, but also because the factory was in Wales, where Pembrokeshire Corgi pedigree dogs were national emblems.*

*The facing page
shows two Land Rovers, a very
popular car in the English countryside of which
numerous versions exist, such as this "Vote for Corgi" model. Above,
under reference number 486, is a Chevrolet Impala from 1959
converted into a kennel service wagon. The canine race is certainly
part and parcel of Corgi creations.*

*Morestone
brought out this police Wolseley toppec
by two enormous sirens. There is a
marvelous illustration on the box showing the
police at the scene of a smash-and-grab raid.*

*These two Dinky Toys were
specially created by Meccano
England for the Swiss market. The
model on the right has fixed doors and
hoods, whereas they are working features of the model on the left.
A disadvantage of opening doors is that they make the car look rather
rugged, as the door pillars are naturally thicker to withstand constant
handling. It is worth pointing out that this VW version, reference
number 262, may appear with other insignia, including this German
mail label.*

*The first cars created by Tekno were*
*Volkswagen, followed by the Ford Taunus and*
*the Volvo PV544, so well-known in Northern Europe.*
*It seems that this taxi, based on the American Ford*
*and created by Tekno in 1959, may have either Taxi*
*or Taxa written on its side.*

*The Australian firm*
*Micromodels had a very short production period,*
*three years at most, between 1958 and 1960. This Holden*
*taxi was released in 1959, and police, pick-up, and van*
*versions of it exist. Note that Holden, part of General*
*Motors, is one of the few car firms to be found in*
*Australia. What is more, this car took much of its*
*inspiration from the American Buicks of the late 1940s.*

*Based on the*
*Taunus 17M, Tekno created this*
miniature with a flashing light, reminiscent of a police car. It used
the same box as the Ford 17M coupé, as shown by the illustration
on the side. Its reference number, with or without a flashing light,
is 826 and it was released in 1962.

*Dinky Toys created
a taxi version of this Opel Rekord
sedan, specifically for the German market. It has been
allocated number 546 in the Meccano numbering. We should
note that the civilian version of this Rekord is number 554.*

Out of all the miniatures in this book my
real passion is for this Plymouth Taxi, launched in 1960, which I
did not even know existed. Created for the American market, this
car was bought by a keen collector in 1962 in Oran. By some
twist of fate it managed to find its way to a shop in Algeria. The
decals on this model were changed at a later stage, and it was
eventually made only in yellow with a red roof.

*Once the French
taxi firm G7 no longer used the
Panhard Z, it was equipped with a fleet of
Peugeot 403 models, followed later by the 404. Dinky Toys
created a stunning replica of this taxi with, as you can see, a
working roof and number plates ending in 75, for Paris. You
might not have known that G7 was named after the Marne area,
denoted by the letter G, where some taxis were registered, and
the number 7, which referred to the region of the Seine.*

*It was only right that the
famous London taxi should also take
its place in the Dinky Toys range. This it did in
1951 with this 40 H Austin Metropolitan, later
renumbered 254. This two-tone car was also
available in either yellow or black.*

*Everyone
knows how fond small
children are of fire engines, as well as Citroëns in general, so it
is not at all surprising then that this 2CV, listed in the Dinky
catalogue of 1958 under reference number 25 D, should have
been such a huge hit. On the right is a 2CV van in plastic,
designed by Norev. The international collectors' magazine,
L'Argus de la Miniature, in issue 164, features no fewer than
18 versions of this standard 1960s van in the liveries of
marques such as Calor, Cibié, Cusenier, Laden, and Teppaz.*

A bonus with
these J.R.D. models,
whether it is the version for
Paris firefighters or French
electricity, is the tiny extending
metal ladder on the roof. This is an
accessory that might easily go astray, but today it is absolutely
indispensable to any self-respecting collector. These miniatures
were released in 1958.

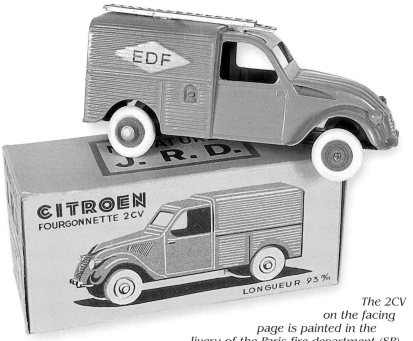

*The 2CV
on the facing
page is painted in the
livery of the Paris fire department (SP).
That model and the one above are in mazac,
whereas J.R.D. is well known for
manufacturing various toy cars in sheet metal.*

*Owning a car is all very well, but if it is new and boxed it is so much better! If there is a choice between contents and container, the greatest rarity value is more often than not to be found in this box made of yellow cardboard…*

*With the growing custom of young people exchanging visits, many English Dinky Toys were taken to France, and other countries, for that matter. So it was that this superb Morris 10 cwt delivery truck ended up in Paris. Page 324 features a version in the livery of the British Royal Mail service.*

*Any joint project between Dinky Toys and Citroën always resulted in tremendous success. And it was no different for this chevron 1200 kg "Tub." It appeared in 1954 with the number 25 C, in the basic version of metallic gray with no lettering. Then a promotional version for the Charles Gervais brand appeared in 1957. Finally, the "Tub" could be found in the Cibié livery, reference 561 in the catalogue of 1959.*

*This Esso van, released in
1950, was a bestseller in Britain and had a very
long production run. This Trojan, a British marque from
Croydon, Surrey, built motorized vehicles between
1928 and 1965. With Dinky reference number 450,
it had several variations, in particular, in the liveries
of Oxo, Cydrax, or Brooke Bond Tea.*

Here is the Royal Mail
van, in its beautiful bright
red paintwork. Released
individually in 1955, this van was also part of
a gift set, made in their usual stylish fashion by Dinky
Toys Liverpool. In addition to this Morris 10 cwt, it
comprised a telephone box, two Post Office figures, as
well as a Post Office telephones van, seen on the facing
page. This gift set is numbered 299.

*Available in 1955, under
reference number 261, was this miniature Morris
van, which was very popular with its roof ladder. Note that
Dinky produced several Austin versions of promotional vans in
the 470 series, including Raleigh Cycles and Nestlé.*

*Familiar
with the infatuation of the
young for Citroën, the French firm Norev
produced many models of this marque. Here is
a police patrol Citroën DS in plastic, a variation of
the civilian sedan. Issued in 1969, it was allocated number 158
by the manufacturer. A French state police version was also made.*

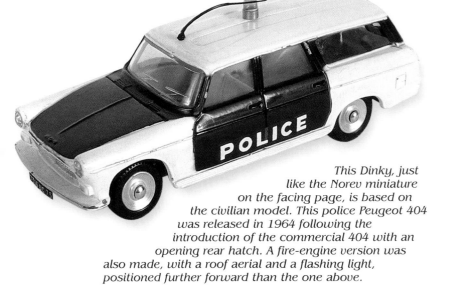

*This Dinky, just like the Norev miniature on the facing page, is based on the civilian model. This police Peugeot 404 was released in 1964 following the introduction of the commercial 404 with an opening rear hatch. A fire-engine version was also made, with a roof aerial and a flashing light, positioned further forward than the one above.*

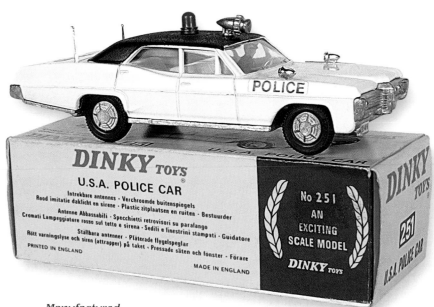

Manufactured
by Dinky Toys in England from
1970, mainly for the American market, is this
US police car, number 251. Notice the variety of intricate
accessories adorning this car: two rear aerials, a flashing light, a
siren, and two cone-shaped rear-vision mirrors!

*Modeled on the Ford Taunus 17M sedan, this Dinky car was reserved for the German market.*

*In 1967
an Italian car was listed in the
Dinky Toys catalogue, which was an
unusual occurrence. This Fiat 2300 station
wagon, number 281, had Pathé News decals and included this
cameraman perched on its roof.*

*This special DS, belonging to the President of the French Republic,
did not have the success anticipated at the time, no doubt because
it was too expensive. It is a replica of the car nicknamed 1 PR 75,
its registration number. It was created for General de Gaulle in 1968
by the coachbuilder, Henri Chapron. In 1970 it was the next President,
Georges Pompidou, who used it. The miniature was distributed
at the Elysée Palace in Paris over Christmas 1970.*

It cannot be stressed enough that all these commercial cars existed only in ID versions, never DS ones. In addition to its typically British cars, Corgi produced a fair number of DS and ID models for its home market, but also for overseas ones such as South Africa. Pictured here is a station wagon kitted out for safari in that far-off land. It is numbered 475-1b, issued in 1964.

*Distributed from 1965, this alpine rescue Citroën ID
in Swiss livery is also a Corgi miniature, from the same
casting as the car on the facing page. Note that Corgi
produced the DS and ID as early as 1957, as well as
many other Citroën models, such as the 2CV, the SM,
and even a Chapron.*

We could devote a whole book to army vehicles alone.
Here is a very rare SR self-propelled tracked machine
gun from 1930. Note that the approximate scale seems
to be 1:50.

In 1964 Meccano invested huge resources in the production of army vehicles. This Panhard FL 11 armored reconnaissance car, issued that year, takes its turret from the AMX tank, released in 1958 by the same manufacturer. Its Dinky reference number is 827 and it was produced during the years 1964 to 1971.

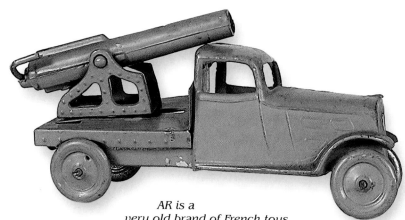

AR is a
very old brand of French toys,
created around 1920. In the mid-1930s
it produced this gun carrier on a Peugeot 301 lead
chassis. Other models may have a searchlight, a tank,
or a van instead of the gun. There even existed a glass
truck version, much sought after today.

*Dinky Toys Liverpool
created some quite striking military vehicles.
Here is a Morris reconnaissance car, Dinky
Toys reference number 152 B, from 1937.*

The Jeep, offering total freedom of mobility, was idolized worldwide. Exactly 663,344 examples were built and we can safely say that the number of its miniature replicas far exceeded this figure! This particular steel model by the firm Polichinelle, kitted out as a fire engine, is very rare, especially in its original box.

As the picture on the box clearly shows, the Willys Jeep by Dinky Toys was sold with a driver. This model was built by Meccano from 1959 to 1963 under reference number 80 B, according to the new numbering system.

*This Corgi Toys civilian version
was available before the Royal Air
Force model, reference number 352, was
put on the miniature cars market in 1958. It
is a Standard Vanguard, an old marque from Coventry, created
in 1903. Beware, though, as no fewer than 11 marques named
Standard are found in England, as well as in the United States,
Germany, and Italy.*

*Four army personnel
may be seen inside this
Oldsmobile Super 88 in
headquarters livery. This very realistic
miniature delighted children who lived near
American army camps. It was launched in
1965 by Corgi, under reference number 358.*

*This Willys Jeep, reference number 814, produced in 1958, is the work of Tekno. Schoolboys of the time were spoilt for choice, as numerous versions existed, including farm, navy, Red Cross, and lastly, military police liveries. The boxes were identical for all models, with one side depicting the military police and the other the farm Jeep.*

*Present-day models are far from
reaching the realism of their 1970s counterparts.
Here is a Delahaye soft-drinks delivery truck, Type
163, from 1948, which features in the current
Minitrucks catalogue.*

*The Citroën T23 was used in virtually*
*every way imaginable by C.I.J. The wheels are*
*in lead, the chassis in steel, but the body, the tipper,*
*and the petrol tank wagon on the facing page are*
*in plaster and flour. Note that a range of fire engines*
*was also created on this casting.*

C.I.J. produced Citroën toys by using various materials such as lithographed sheet metal, papier mâché, celluloid, lead, and even a mixture of plaster and flour. These two lorries are made from this last combination.

*After manufacturing Citroën toys, C.I.J. turne[d]*
*its interests to building Renault toys. Here a[re]*
*two examples of these toys made fro[m]*
*plaster and flour, dating from the late 1930[s].*

Several models were available: a cattle truck with two cows, a brewery version with an open wagon of 24 racks of beer bottles, and two more tankers for cattle feed and petrol.

*This 1:45 semi-trailer truck by J.R.D. is a Citroën 23 from 1936.*
*It was given different types of trailer. We should note that it is*
*made from plaster and flour, with steel fenders.*

Here is the chassis of the truck on the right. Apart
from its method of construction, there is lettering
to indicate that it was manufactured in France by
Meccano. In spite of its broken front bumper,
observe the pristine condition for a toy of this age.

*The first trucks manufactured by Dinky Toys did not resemble any particular truck, but looked generally like a typical heavy truck of the period. This charming miniature truck, reference number 25, was made in several versions with Esso, Essolube, and Standard liveries, and even one with a working tipper.*

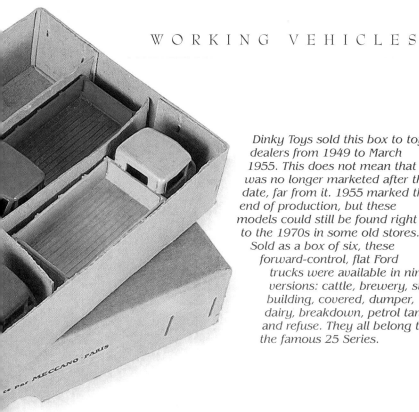

Dinky Toys sold this box to toy dealers from 1949 to March 1955. This does not mean that it was no longer marketed after that date, far from it. 1955 marked the end of production, but these models could still be found right up to the 1970s in some old stores. Sold as a box of six, these forward-control, flat Ford trucks were available in nine versions: cattle, brewery, site building, covered, dumper, dairy, breakdown, petrol tank, and refuse. They all belong to the famous 25 Series.

It was no doubt because US army surplus was teeming with these Studebaker trucks that Dinky had the idea of modeling them in miniature. Conceived as early as 1948, they arrived on the market the following year, and did not leave it before 1954. This model, reference number 25 M, is equipped with a trailer hook.

*The Studebaker truck was made in nine versions. Whereas the truck on the facing page had a manual tipper, this one was a covered version, reference 25 Q.*

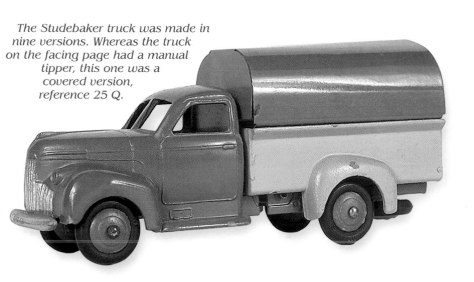

*This miniature trailer created by Meccano England was put on sale in 1954. At that time, the front axle pin was visible on the floor, as may be seen from the picture on the box. After 1960, this pin was no longer noticeable.*

This Austin covered wagon
from Dinky Toys Liverpool, reference
number 413, was introduced in 1954.
The cover was not made of canvas,
but of sturdy steel.

The *Argus de la Miniature* allocates reference number 3–20 for this petrol tanker that the firm C.I.J. sold from 1951 onward. It is a Panhard truck from 1948, with forward control, which was a new fashion at the time. Note that the first models were furnished with "Energic BP Energol" decals, as inscribed on the box on the left, and not "Energol BP Energol," as above. Energic was the trade name for British Petroleum gasoline, and Energol, its engine oil.

*Simca manufactured
this cargo truck that was modeled
in miniature by Dinky Toys at
Bobigny, therefore establishing its
popularity. Reference 33 B was the
dumper truck and 33 A the glass
version. A third Dinky model, numbered
33 AN, replicated a yellow removal truck in Bailly livery.
Note that Dinky Toys marketed over 1,000 items from the
period 1933-34, and that Meccano ceased to exist in
France in 1972 and seven years later in England.*

*Certainly one of the finest and most spectacular 1:43 trucks is this Berliet created by Meccano France. Issued in 1955 under reference number 34 A, its dumper is a copy of the Marrel model, controlled by a small chrome handle. An identical Berliet in a container version was available from 1956.*

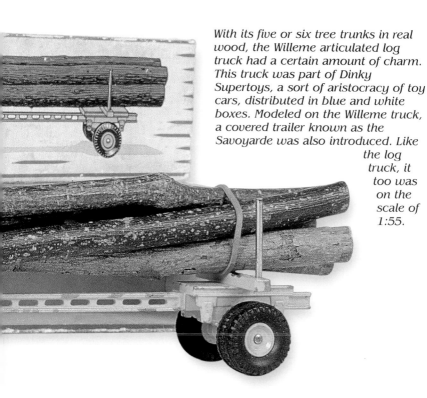

With its five or six tree trunks in real wood, the Willeme articulated log truck had a certain amount of charm. This truck was part of Dinky Supertoys, a sort of aristocracy of toy cars, distributed in blue and white boxes. Modeled on the Willeme truck, a covered trailer known as the Savoyarde was also introduced. Like the log truck, it too was on the scale of 1:55.

*There is little information on this 29 B bu
found in the Dinky Toys catalogue of 193(
The first models have a small square re;
windou*

In blue and silver
or red and silver, the Isobloc bus, Dinky
Toys reference number 29 E, was typical of the
1950s. On its launch, from 1951, it had neither a ridged
roof nor embossed sides, in which case the fender cutouts
were stencil-plated.

Modeled on the Panhard Movic articulated truck, Dinky Toys
created three trucks, including this tanker with Esso decals,
designed for fueling airplanes. The other articulated trucks were
in the liveries of Kodak and the SNCF French railways.

*You would have to be English to create the model for this Coventry Climax forklift truck, but the French borrowed the casting and the truck was also produced at Bobigny. In England, its production began in 1949 under reference number 14 C, but in France it was allocated number 597 and manufactured from 1959 to 1961.*

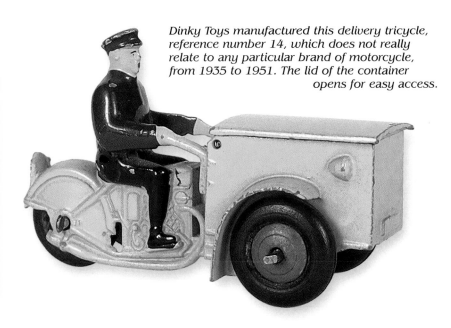

*Dinky Toys manufactured this delivery tricycle, reference number 14, which does not really relate to any particular brand of motorcycle, from 1935 to 1951. The lid of the container opens for easy access.*

# Index
# Bibliography
# Addresses
# Acknowledgments

# Index

This index includes the principal proper names
and marques cited in this book.

# INDEX

# *Bibliography*

Ames, Bob. *Vintage Miniature Racing Cars.*
United States: Graphic Arts Center Pub, 1992.

Force, Edward. *Dinky Toys.*
United States: Shiffer Publishing, 2002.

Mack, Charlie. *Encyclopedia of Matchbox Toys 1947-1996.*
United States: Shiffer Publishing, 1999.

Rampini, Paolo. *The Golden Book of Model Cars, 1900–1975.*
Italy: published by the author, 1995.

Richardson, Mike and Sue. *Dinky Toys and Modelled Miniatures.*
England: New Cavendish Books, 1986.

Richardson, Mike. *Collecting Dinky Toys.*
England: Francis Joseph Publications, 2001.

Stephen, Elizabeth A. *Today's Hottest Die-cast Vehicles.*
United States: Krause Publications, 2000.

# Addresses

## United States

Christie's
20, Rockerfeller Plaza
New York NY 10021
Tel: 212 636 2000
www.christies.com
Contact: Toys department

Sotheby's
1334, York Avenue
New York, NY 10021
Tel: 212 606 7000
www.sothebys.com
Contact: Toys and dolls department

Diecast Car Collector's Club
PO Box 670226
Los Angeles CA 90067-1126
www.diecast.org

Dinky Toy Club of America
PO Box 11
Highland
Maryland 20777
Tel: 301 854 2217
Contact: Jerry Fralick

## Great Britain

Christie's
85, Old Brompton Road
London SW7 3LD
Tel: 0207 581 7611
www.christies.com
Contact: Hugo Marsh

Vectis Auctions Ltd. (Sotheby's)
Fleck Way, Thornaby,
Stockton-on-Tees TS17 957
Tel: 01642 750 616
www.vectis.co.uk

Cotswold Motoring Museum and Toy
Collection
Shelbourne Street
Bourton-on-the-Water
Gloucestershire GL54 2BY
Tel: 01451 821 255

Coventry Toy Museum
Whitefriars Gate
Much Park Street
Coventry CV1 2LT
Tel: 01203 227 560

# Useful Web sites

www.collectiques.net  
www.corgi.co.uk  
www.diecastminiatures.com  
www.diecastreplicas.com  
www.dinkycollector.com  

www.ebay.com  
www.matchboxclub.com  
www.minicastcars.com  
www.modelcars.co.uk  
www.swapmeet.co.uk  

# Acknowledgments

*I would like to thank those people who have helped to make this work possible by entrusting me with their treasured miniatures and lending me their advice. The following list is in no particular order:*

*Philippe Lepage (Le Petit Mayet); Etienne Flament; François Binetruy (Brocante de l'Orangerie); Jean-Jacques Ehrlacher; Franck Schaefer; Jacques de Riedmatten; Jean-Claude Puaud; Claire Ducamp.*

*And thank you to my big sister, Geneviève, who, each time she returned from one of her language-learning trips to Birmingham, never forgot to bring me back one or two of those magical yellow boxes.*

## In the same series

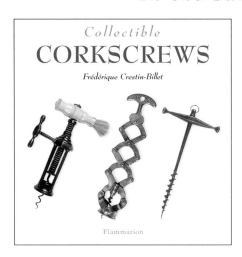

Collectible Corkscrews
by Frédérique Crestin-Billet

Collectible Pocket Knives
by Dominique Pascal

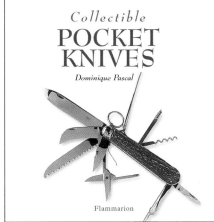

*Collectible Miniature
Perfume Bottles*
by Anne Breton

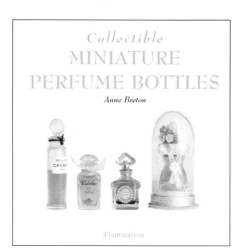

*Collectible Wristwatches*
by René Pannier

# Photographic credits

FA0718-02-II
Dépôt légal: April 2002